Preaching to a World in Crisis

Preaching to a World in Crisis
Sermons by Horton Davies

Edited By
HENRY BOWDEN
AND
MARIE-HÉLÈNE DAVIES

WIPF & STOCK · Eugene, Oregon

PREACHING TO A WORLD IN CRISIS
Sermons by Horton Davies

Copyright © 2009 Marie-Hélène Davies. All rights reserved. Except for brief quotations in critical publications or reviews, no part of this book may be reproduced in any manner without prior written permission from the publisher. Write: Permissions, Wipf and Stock, 199 W. 8th Ave., Suite 3, Eugene, OR 97401.

Wipf and Stock Publishers
199 W. 8th Ave., Suite 3
Eugene, OR 97401

www.wipfandstock.com

ISBN 13: 978-1-60608-151-8

Manufactured in the U.S.A.

To George Reginald Bishop, Jr.
Who, late in life,
Still prepares the way for the Lord.

Contents

Foreword / ix

Acknowledgements / xi

Introduction: Contexts for the Sermons / 1

1 The Perils of Our Calling / 25

PART ONE: Preaching During World War II

2 Citizens of Two Kingdoms / 31

3 Harvest Festival / 35

4 The Shepherds, the Scientists, and Simeon / 40

5 The Modernity of the Master / 46

6 Absolute Loyalty / 53

7 Let My People Go / 57

8 The Persistence of Goodness in an Evil World / 62

9 Modern Madness and the Cure of Christ / 65

10 Nailing Our Colors to the Mast / 70

11 Retrospect / 76

12 Christianity in the Atomic Age / 82

13 No Apologies / 86

14 Eternal Life: Heaven and Hell / 91

15 Christ and Individual Need (1) / 97

16 Christ and Individual Need (2): Thou and They / 100

PART TWO: Preaching in a World in Crisis (South Africa)

17 The Rightful Claims of Heaven and Earth / 107

18 Resolution: A New Year Sermon, 1950 / 113

19 Race-Tensions in South Africa / 117

20 *Resurgam* / 131

PART THREE: Preaching in a World in Crisis (America)

21 Communion Devotion: The Realism of the Gospel / 137

22 Dangerous Silence / 141

23 The Threat of Secularism / 146

24 The Gospel and the Reversal of Human Values / 151

25 A Victorious Faith Conquering Prejudice / 156

26 The World Church and Human Need / 161

27 Protests, Profound, and Trivial / 168

28 Hoping against Hope / 175

PART FOUR: Jesus: *Monarch of Men*

29 Jesus Baptized / 183

30 Jesus the Evangelist / 188

31 Jesus, Social Thinker / 193

32 Jesus, Man of Prayer / 198

33 Jesus Enthroned / 203

Foreword

It is an honor for me to write a foreword to this second collection of sermons by Horton Davies which were delivered during the years of World War II, crisis in South Africa, and crisis in the USA. This latest volume succeeds the first volume of sermons entitled *Believing* which was edited by John Booty and Marie-Hélène Davies. To be found in the previous volume is a masterful review of the sermons by Horton Davies, organized under the headings of the Creed. This second volume of sermons goes hand in hand with the first.

I was introduced to Horton Davies over forty years ago when he led a clergy conference of the Episcopal Church in Delaware. I vividly remember his presence, especially in the way he captured the imagination of those present from the minute he began to speak. It was clear to all of us that this was not going to be just another leader at a required meeting of clergy!

Recalling the spiritual depth of Dr. Davies which penetrated his words and guided the discussion from start to finish, it was fortunate for me to see him again after moving to Princeton years later. It was a privilege for me in his retirement to have opportunities to speak informally with him after services in the church we attended. Those occasions reminded me of the great contributions he made to theology and historical research over a long life.

Although his vast learning and years as a teacher and preacher were on my mind whenever I spoke with him, there was one attribute that escaped me until I read a book he edited in 1990: *The Communion of Saints, Prayers of the Famous*. It was the place of spirituality in his life. His collection of prayers, favorite ones for him over the years, pointed to an interior life, which manifested itself in his research, teaching, and preaching. The book opened up for me a whole side of his life, which only focussing on his academic skills could not. The book of prayers of the famous pointed to the key relationship between spirituality and preaching—

the spirituality of the preacher—the importance of, and the connection between, the word spoken and the conviction behind it.

To illustrate such connection, three references to prayers found in *The Communion of Saints, Prayers of the Famous* will reveal the spirituality of Horton Davies. The first is the familiar words of John Donne about grace:

> Batter my heart, three person'd God; for you
> As yet but knock, breathe, shine, and seek to mend
> That I may rise, and stand, o'erthrow me, and bend
> Your force to break, blow, burn, and make me new.

The second: Cardinal Newman's words of trust: "O Lord, support us all the day long, until the shadows lengthen and the evening comes, and the busy world is hushed, and the fever of life is over, and our work is done. Then in your mercy grant us a safe lodging, and a holy rest, and peace at the last."

The third: Dag Hammarksjöld's petition:

> Give us a pure heart that we may see you,
> A humble heart that we may hear you,
> A heart of love that we may serve you,
> A heart of faith that we may abide in you

In the introduction to his book on prayers, Horton Davies refers to the New Testament interpretation of being "called to be saints" which he describes as a matter of "intention rather than achievement." His choices of prayers that make up the book are offered to encourage beginners as well as to comfort experienced followers of Christ. Rereading his words about Christian spirituality was further evidence for me of the spirituality of Horton Davies, as it was revealed continuously throughout his life, in his writing and preaching.

G. P. Mellick Belshaw
IX Bishop, Episcopal Diocese of New Jersey

Acknowledgements

After working together on *Believing*, the first volume of sermons by Horton Davies, published by Wipf and Stock, John Booty and I considered publishing a homiletical sequel, centered around history. It is therefore he, who chose many of the sermons, whom I want to thank first. Unfortunately, because of health problems, Dr. Booty was unable to complete the work with me. I then turned for support to Mellick Belshaw, formerly bishop of New Jersey and a member of Trinity Church, Princeton. Not only did he agree to write a foreword to the volume, but he also furnished me with precious advice on how to introduce the sermons, to give the reader context. Finally, the present editor, Dr. Henry Bowden, a former student of Horton Davies at Princeton and a retired member of the Religion Department at Rutgers University, generously offered his expertise. He helped with the final selection and ordering of the sermons and wrote a scholarly and warm introduction laying out the historical events and biographical details that gave birth to the sermons.

We also want to thank Jean Hadidian and Susan Manchester for their professional editing, the staff and typesetter of Wipf and Stock for bringing the book to the finish, and Princeton University for its support in this labor of love and remembrance. To all we are profoundly grateful.

Introduction

Contexts for the Sermons

IN 1942, WHEN HORTON DAVIES was ordained and installed as pastor of the Congregational Church in Wallington, a suburban community south of London, he had already obtained two degrees from the University of Edinburgh and was within a year of earning his doctorate from Mansfield College, Oxford University. Training in theology and homiletics had prepared him well for eloquent preaching and the cure of souls amid the hectic pace of modern life around London. But by 1942 circumstances had introduced new anxieties and spiritual burdens to all of those in the parish he had come to serve. England had been at war with Germany for almost three years, and the towns of Wallington and nearby Carshalton were adjacent to Croydon airport. Thus they were vulnerable targets in the irregular but still destructive bombing raids that the Luftwaffe continued to conduct over the metropolitan area. The specter of imminent death was an additional challenge that a new cleric, fresh from school, had to cope with, alongside the more everyday circumstances that called for counseling. Davies's sermons of that early time responded heroically to the psychological stress attendant upon daily worry about incendiary bombs, and concerns about family members serving in the military.

Torments of that sort were rife and deeply seated. When German forces swept west in early 1940, the outmanned contingent of British soldiers in France were overwhelmed, escaping annihilation at Dunkirk in late May. Thereafter the chief of German air power was determined to take the war over the English Channel and weaken the islanders' will to fight, prior to invasion. Saturation bombing of air fields, industrial cities, and especially London, colloquially known as "the Blitz," took a heavy toll in lives and property. Indeed, the havoc wreaked by Luftwaffe bombing raids inflicted the greatest destruction in areas of London known to history. More than thirty thousand people were killed during those harrowing months, and another fifty thousand were injured. Still, the Royal Air Force beat back the onslaught, lessened the intensity and frequency of raids, and, by the early months of 1941, had virtually won the "Battle of Britain." But sporadic bombings continued, all the more unsettling because of their unpredictability.

Such hectic times placed heavy burdens on Wallington residents, forcing them to live with uncertainty, respond at once to warning sirens at all hours, and take shelter where they could find it. The weight of woe and foreboding was hardly bearable. Toward the end of the war German tactics changed to using rockets instead of airplanes. The V1 rocket was a flying bomb twenty-five feet long with a one-ton explosive warhead that traveled at four hundred miles per hour. It was not very accurate but terribly destructive wherever it happened to fall. Davies's parish of Wallington experienced well over a hundred of these random bombings, one of which exploded in a school playground, killing several children. German ingenuity then produced the V2, a more sophisticated weapon that flew faster than sound and fell without warning on, among others, citizens in Surrey, south of London.

Amid these harrowing circumstances the twenty-four year old minister preached sermons that emphasized hope, betterment, and renewal. He encouraged families who had sons who were prisoners of war to remain steadfast in hope for their survival and release. He offered consolation and compassion to those who were afflicted with troubles closer at hand. He used biblical themes to call for the invasion of the continent, the defeat of Nazi evil, and the resurgence of goodness in people that might help them to rise above the thrall of wartime conditions. He organized Bible study groups in local homes, both for better understanding of Scripture and for mutual encouragement among those depressed by international hostilities. During the immense conflicts of World War II he sensed that individual parishioners were feeling increasingly hollow, diminished, and insignificant. They seemed depressed by a sense of threats all around them, despondent over the random patterns of violence that rained on them from the skies. As a cure to this mild form of mental illness, his sermons lifted up courage and patience founded on faith in Christ. Good would triumph over evil, he promised, conquering the inward forms of it as well as the outer ones.

In addition to buttressing faith and stability within his congregation, Davies also denounced Nazi violation of human rights, particularly the diabolical persecution of Jews, dissecting the historical, sociological, and psychological causes for such an abomination. He also drew a parallel between those who blindly followed the Führer and the ancient Israelites who angered God by worshipping the golden calf. In a context larger than just contemporary politics he scrutinized modern psychological tensions manifested by virtually everyone, especially those who taxed peace of mind in pursuit of "success." To counter this malady he offered a Christian ideal of wholeness through service, an end to fear and frustration, and incidentally an antidote to forms of anti-Semitism that lurked to some degree in every Christian heart. The best life, he urged, was one that served God by serving others. It was not one that pursued money, fame, or even security. It was not a life of apprehension. Even in humility the Christ-like life was heroic.

While still in his first pastorate, but thinking beyond the focus of wartime anxieties, Davies also spoke to conditions endemic to modern life, irenic as well as bellicose. He knew that people were searching for answers about life in the context of evolutionary science in an at least partially rational universe. He spoke often of accepting scientific discoveries, of shunning both racist attitudes and those of social snobbery too. The Christian life, he proclaimed, was one of manifesting God's Word through service to neighbors. The open and determined witness to Christ's Gospel was one that could overcome physical hardships and overcome the psychological dread of death. The events of Good Friday pointed to resurrection, and this in turn fostered progress in this world as well as everlasting life in the time to come. Thus modern man was released from guilt and was able to rise above sadness, perplexity, and rootless boredom.

The year 1947 brought great change, both geographically and professionally. Davies accepted an appointment as Professor of Divinity at Rhodes University College in Grahamstown, Union of South Africa. He faced the stimulating task of inaugurating a new academic discipline at that institution, a task that started with supplementing the college library's meager holdings relevant to theological education. Within a short period of time he fashioned a curriculum that featured studies in Old Testament, New Testament, Systematic Theology, and Church history. This solid orientation won the approval of university regents and also attracted talented part-time lecturers to flesh out the teaching program. There were three extant Afrikaans seminaries for which Davies was also responsible, but Rhodes was the first English-medium college in South Africa that trained future English-speaking ministers. As the program expanded, Davies became dean of its faculty in 1951 and remained at that post until he made another career move two years later.

Any sensitive newcomer to South Africa was immediately struck by the strong contrasts prevailing there. Davies was quite favorably impressed with the university's grand architecture and by the impressive housing available to White residents. But he was equally appalled to observe the ramshackle housing of a social class called "Coloreds" and the even more miserable huts of native Africans. The regnant class system, usually known as "apartheid," was one of open discrimination by a minority of Whites against all others. At the midpoint of the last century South Africa contained approximately thirty million inhabitants, officially divided into classes by the Population Registration Act of 1950. Of that total a mere five million Whites (descendents mostly of Dutch and British) held rigorous dominion over twenty-one million Blacks (predominantly Zulus and Xhosas), three million Coloreds (most of them Cape Malays), and one million Asians (essentially immigrants from India).

The Union of South Africa had come into being in 1910, but the attitudes and practices of racial segregation had begun much earlier than that. It had long been the policy of Afrikaner churchmen and legislators to maintain territorial as well as social separation of the races who lived in the region. This fundamental discrimination resulted in complete domination of state and society by the White population. For example the vote was denied to all non-White men, not to mention women of any sort. Marriage between Whites and non-Whites, indeed any form of sexual relations, were declared illegal by the Mixed Marriages Act of 1949 and the Immorality Act of 1950. By a law sanctioned in the Group Areas Act of 1950, native Africans were allowed to own land only in the Native Reserves (Bantu Homelands), an area that made up only 13% of the surface that constituted South African holdings. Within that small territory, overcrowded and living in rural slums while at the same time burdened with poverty and taxation, natives ostensibly enjoyed a measure of political and economic freedom. But even there liberty was limited and fragile because any internally generated action by natives could be vetoed by the president of South Africa. All remunerative vocations in industry and management were reserved for Whites, while the deliberately less educated non-Whites had to settle for menial jobs and remain subservient. Native workers were required to obtain passes in order to enter White farmlands or to remain for any length of time in urban areas. They were literally regarded as aliens, temporarily present in White society, tolerated there only as long as they were docile and kept their place.

Sermons composed during the South Africa years often alluded to the disgrace of apartheid. They offered no simple solutions to the highly complex factors that underlay the often brutal oppression of native peoples, but Davies repeatedly preached the brotherhood of all races and called for courageous, creative change. He criticized Churches for enjoying central prominence as pillars of social eminence while remaining acquiescent in racial segregation and ineffective in socio-economic issues. In thoughtful, measured terms he analyzed the tangled skein of prejudice and precedent that had produced contemptible abuses. Then he called for nothing less than a change of heart and mind among White Christians, those strategically placed to effect reform. Just as the London sermons invoked biblical examples and doctrine, so the South African sermons also called for a rigorous pursuit of a Christ-like lifestyle, especially as it applied to redressing evil in the temporal world.

In 1953 Davies became chairman of the Congregational Union of South Africa, a consortium composed primarily of Congregational Churches, but one that exhibited a wider ecumenical outreach as well. In that capacity he often visited Black churches and noted that native ecclesiastical structures afforded a much greater degree of understanding and compassion than was granted to native Christians in national life. He was also gratified to receive a warm welcome and genuine acceptance within native congregations, more that he expected as a Caucasian ... and more than he received in some circles of Whites. Davies earned the disapproval of many by speaking out so forthrightly against apartheid. Nevertheless he urged Church leaders, especially those associated with the Union he administered, to fight for social and ethnic justice.

The struggle, he knew, would be long and bitter because the entrenched White minority would not easily give up its political and economic privileges. So his sermons of this period sought to balance the mundane and the eternal. He hoped to help believers to cope with problems endemic to their own mortality by emphasizing increased trust in God. By stressing the perennial constants of justice, faith, and charity, he tried to diminish personal insecurities while at the same time encourage commitment to struggles against institutionalized forms of hatred, greed, and the abuse of power. A victorious faith could, he held, conquer egotistic paralysis, prejudice, and vindictiveness. A life of service to others led to forgiveness among all concerned, which in turn pointed ahead to resurrection and eternal life,

Negative reactions to anti-apartheid activities were at least one consideration in the decision to leave South Africa in 1953. Another cause had to do with a more basic reorientation in vocational perspective. From 1953 to 1956 Davies returned to England and served as senior lecturer in ecclesiastical history at Mansfield and Regents Park Colleges, Oxford. In that capacity he deepened his long-standing interests in ecumenical developments while also exploring new ways of understanding theology through scrutinizing various forms of worship. Research and publication in these fields led in 1956 to his appointment as Professor of Religion at Princeton University in the United States, a position he occupied for twenty-eight years until his retirement in 1984.

The study of religion at major American universities was developing an interesting new perspective by the time Davies arrived on the scene. In previous decades the study of different religious topics was almost always intended to prepare men and women for vocations as ordained ministers or for other forms of church work. Information and exercises were experienced in a context of advocacy and concerns for "orthodoxy," however a particular seminary tended to define that term. Such curricula served the enhancement of religious life, leadership, and beneficial effect of the world at large. In the second half of the twentieth century many American scholars began moving away from studying religion for religious purposes, preferring instead to study it for academic ones. The key difference was non-committal objectivity instead of evangelical advocacy, a more detached attempt to learn about religion rather than to advocate any particular form of it. Programs with this orientation were first promulgated in Ivy League schools and then spread to other major educational establishments. Many observers made the distinction institutionally, not accurate in every instance but used nevertheless, by equating the traditional approach with theological seminaries and locating the new perspective in secular universities.

When Davies arrived at Princeton, its more academic approach to religion studies was relatively new, put into place only a few years earlier. He enthusiastically endorsed the intention of showing, by means of both undergraduate lectures and graduate seminars alike, how religion was relevant to the larger circles of social and cultural life. His classes with undergraduate attendees were an immediate success, enrolling upwards of fifty students per course. This new program quickly attracted national attention on the graduate level as well, drawing an average of one hundred applications each year to a program that could only admit eight or nine new doctoral aspirants. In a short time the Princeton curriculum expanded its objective, inclusive viewpoint by including such topics as Judaism, Hinduism, Buddhism, and other Asian religions in addition to the more familiar subjects of biblical studies, philosophy, ethics, and Church history. Beyond that, the doctoral program also insisted that candidates pass proficiency tests in two languages other than English and take at least two seminars in a university department outside their own—history, Philosophy and Near Eastern languages being the most frequently chosen. The approach was broad; the standards were rigorous.

Secular standards were centered on the rational analysis of physical evidence of a human, mundane provenance. If people believed that God had performed a certain miracle, it was acceptable to regard human expressions of that belief as historical fact. Whether or not God had actually acted in that manner was irrelevant to the new secular approach because it pertained to a transcendent, not a mundane, category. Studying people who acted in the name of Jehovah, or Allah, or Buddha, was a legitimate pursuit, compatible with other topics in the realm of secular learning. Trying to verify the existence, nature, or intentions of any of these references to the divine was not. Religion was important, in the humanist and secular view, not because it edified souls and communities with spiritual truths but because it had exerted great influence on cultural patterns in every country in every age. Religious factors had affected events of both human cruelty and self-sacrifice, of oppressive wars and pacifist compassion, of artistic creativity and iconoclastic destruction. This perspective about the importance of studying religion within the restrictions of a secularist context was one in which Davies flourished and rose to eminence.

The most important of these genres in which an early interest of his progressed to eminence was that of liturgical studies. Harking back to the days of his own doctoral dissertation, an inquiry into evangelical revivals and worship patterns among English Puritans, Davies had long nurtured a perspective that sought to understand Christian thought through public expressions of the sacred. The first of these avenues was one of the most familiar to him: preaching. He knew that a sermon's structured composition, the occasion on which it was delivered, and the purpose for which it was intended yielded a great deal of relevant information. Those elements shed light on both the speaker who delivered the sermon and the congregation that received it, suggesting future developments that might occur. While probing the characteristics of preaching, Davies moved more deeply into the nature of sacred rhetoric in all its forms. One of these fruitful genres was the varied types of prayers used in churches. And since some prayers were sung, additional inquiry led to studies of hymnody and the place of music in worship. The greatest culmination of such scholarship was his six-volume coverage of liturgical activity in every major Christian denomination in England from the time of the Reformation to the present: *Worship and Theology in England* (1961–1997).

The most elemental forms of public worship included sermons, prayers, and hymns. They also included use of at least two of the traditional sacraments, Baptism and the Eucharist. Whatever the mode of baptism, immersion or pouring, use of the ritual said something about those who employed it. Similarly, various forms of communion, as well as the elements used, shed light on much broader categories in the minds of the participants. Preaching, praying, singing, and sharing the Lord's Supper usually took place indoors, and this led Davies to considerations of architecture. And inquiring into the way a building's design could enhance worship pointed inevitably to what eventually came to be Davies's highest priority: the importance of Christianity to the visual arts. Religious expressions in painting and sculpture had left a rich heritage that stemmed all the way back to apostolic times, and an analysis of those media provided valuable information about the people who created them. They also offered a possible means of understanding the many succeeding generations who continued to find different religious meanings through the accumulated wealth of religious images. One of the most striking contributions from the professor in this area is *Sacred Art in a Secular Century* (1978).

Another major twentieth century trend with which Davies expressed total and enthusiastic support was the growth of ecumenism. Taking a long view, one can say that the modern ecumenical movement began when the International Missionary Council met at Edinburgh (1910). There missionaries deplored the rivalries displayed by emissaries of European Churches as they sought to convert others in foreign countries. Such competition bewildered natives, and it hampered progress. Plans for further meetings were made after the Council in hopes of generating more mutual trust and acceptance in light of the fact that separate institutions were ultimately pursuing the same goals. One of these further steps was a conference on "Life and Work" which first met in Stockholm (1925) to see how separate Churches could combine their efforts to address some of the great social, political, and economic problems that were rife in modern times. Another step was taken by convening a conference on "Faith and Order" in Lausanne (1927). There and in subsequent meetings, different denominations were surprised to learn how ignorant they were about the beliefs and practices of other groups and, upon cordial scrutiny, how much they held in common. Ecumenism reached a higher level in 1948 when mainstream Protestant Churches created the World Council of Churches to promote greater cooperation and unity. It soared even higher in 1965 when Roman Catholics were allowed to participate with permission from the Second Vatican Council.

Discussions about ecumenism tend to fall into one of two groups. All discussants find fault with denominational separatism, but each side sees the problem differently and thus proposes a different solution. On the one hand many ecumenists, including most Americans interested in the subject, see the problem to be one of ignorant suspicion that has led to wasteful competition. Interdenominational rivalries spawned the same agencies and programs in different Churches. This redundancy squandered money and manpower while trying to accomplish the same objectives in society. Squabbling between Churches was bad management; suspicion and distrust was bad faith. The answer for this school of thought was to change attitudes and promote greater cooperation through mutual acceptance of denominational differences, differences that should not prevent mutual efforts to solve common problems. In the United States, the National Council of Churches of 1907 was a good example of this kind of approach. The other school of thought in ecumenical sympathies regards the separation of Churches in much more theological terms. The proliferation of separate Churches is, from this viewpoint, a scandal—a perennial sin. Separatism tears apart the seamless robe of Christ and violates the concept of one faithful people. The solution is easily proposed, difficult though it might be to achieve: delete separate denominations through increasingly comprehensive mergers and reunions. If there is one God and one Christ, there ought to be no more than one Church.

Davies grew up while these ideas were burgeoning; he echoed and exhibited them. While originally associated with the Congregational denomination, one that was categorized as a "Dissenter" sect in earlier English history, he always displayed an understanding of, and empathy with, other confessional groups. He fostered mutual cooperation among Churches in Wallington. In South Africa he sought to correlate interdenominational activities in both education and progressive social change. In America he favored the formation of the United Church of Christ in 1957, a merger between the Congregational Christian Churches and the Evangelical and Reformed Church. Another strong sign of ecumenism which Davies backed was the 1960 Consultation on Church Union, especially its achievement of having Lutheran and Episcopalian ministers share pulpits and altars. The ecclesial events synchronized with his personal convictions and with the conclusions he reached through intensive reading about the past. A wide-ranging ecumenical outlook permeated his academic life, broadened his scholarship, and strengthened his sermons.

Sermons composed in these later years were couched in references to many of the characteristics of modern times. They scrutinized and responded especially to the threats latent in existentialism, communism, and totalitarianism. Davies had always embraced a rigorous theology, and he often referred to the neo-orthodox Karl Barth to articulate views with which he agreed. He considered Barth to be a compatible thinker because both he and the Swiss theologian insisted vigorously on a biblical basis for theology. They were equally unwilling to dilute God's demands placed on a wayward, self-deluded world. As far as existentialism was concerned, Davies tried to expose its ultimate despair that failed to support the human spirit. And contrarily he preached against the hive mentality of communism and the way it destroyed the dignity of each individual. Totalitarian regimes, from Hitler and Stalin to Idi Amin, were ultimately blasphemous because they sought to replace the Almighty as the one supreme absolute. In face of such perversions he reverted to holding up the Reformation concepts of God's forgiveness and justification by faith. While God's Word could not be reduced to a simple humanistic scheme of mundane improvement, he insisted that it could nevertheless heal human despair and also be powerfully beneficial in daily affairs.

Thus ending as he began, persisting through decades of warfare, apartheid, and intellectual broadening through scholarship, Davies proclaimed a gospel of hope against despair. He invoked the good news of forgiveness as he sought to balance the importance of each resurrected individual within the larger context of the whole communion of saints.

And on some bold occasions his ecumenical outreach rose to a pinnacle where he could envision common ground not only among different Christian groups but among agnostics and atheists as well. This extensive, inclusive view of the faith made it powerful enough to embrace all men and women, no matter what their origins and initial experience.

LITERARY COMMENTARY

The previous volume, *Believing*, showed how Davies sharpened the Sword of the Spirit by his discipline of thought, the variety of rhetorical devices, and the wealth of imagination that he used in tempering his sermons. This volume presents the same characteristics, with an evolution in the preacher's craft largely influenced by circumstances, the physical and political geography of his country of residence, and also by the maturation of one, who, having traveled distant lands, rediscovered the eternal truth of God beyond the constraints of location and time. In later years, because of Davies's increasing duties, as founder of the Religion department in South Africa, chairman of the department in Oxford, and professor and graduate representative in America, sermons are less numerous, but they gain the wealth of experience and wisdom that should go with maturity. In common they represent both daring and fear of the judgment of God hand in hand, as Davies preached in Baxter's words "as a dying man to dying men," in awe, lest he should betray the Word of God.

Some sermons were started and then written as sketches, others have the span of Doctrine, Reason and Use with full-fledged examples, rhetorical devices, and imagery. Rarely is Davies at a loss for words, doing thus honor to his Edinburgh degree in B. Lit.; only once, in "The divine overruling" do we feel that he is at his wits' end, stretching his mind and compassion in a desperate effort to comfort those who lost their children in the raid which destroyed a London school. The same feeling of helplessness happened a few years later, when during a summer pastorate in Connecticut, he had to deal the same week with the sorrow of the "friend" of a pilot who crashed, overwhelmed by the questions and concerns of the villagers, and the death of a young boy electrocuted on a fence. As a consoler of the afflicted, Davies felt at a loss for words, and though he did preach a sermon that week, yet there is, up to now, no trace of it in his files. The memory of these three tragedies kept haunting him in later years, as well as the humbling feeling of his own inadequacy.

In "The perils of our calling," Davies maps out the dangers encountered by the hubris of the minister and his formidable endeavors as faithful servant of the Word, bringing, by the sword of the Spirit, a message of peace and love to neighbors.

Sermons, like teaching, seek to illuminate; but they also need to leave an emotional resonance. The preacher addresses not only the intelligence and the memory, but also the heart and imagination. For this he only has some twenty to thirty minutes to make his point memorable. In this historical smorgasbord of sermons, there is a difference of tone in the war sermons of London ranging from compassion to righteous anger both against German cruelty and English governmental apathy. In South Africa, Davies addresses color and colonists' prejudices, whilst praising the progress and modernization of the country, and calls for unity. In America, despite his gratitude for its abundance, generosity, and the allowance for discovery and experimentation, his main concern is human rights and the competition in social status between and within the various denominations of the Church. He therefore moves from the consciousness of the evil without to an awareness of the grey within the Body of Christ, to call Christians to repentance.

The topics and techniques Davies most admired in Homiletics appeared mostly in *Varieties of English Preaching* and in chapter II of *Like Angels from a Cloud* (Huntington Library, San Marino, 1986). There he analyses the eleven main points of metaphysical preaching, which vary according to the preacher's preferences. Some could be used as a base to examine Davies's own sermons. Although a Congregationalist, his training and admiration for English literature prompted him to go beyond the Puritan plain style of Doctrine, Reason and Use, to indulge in variegated colors. *Like Angels from a Cloud* actually argues that many Puritan preachers did adopt a more ornate style.

Important are the titles of the sermons themselves, whether they are direct biblical quotes as in "Let my people go," and "*Resurgam*," or descriptive as in "Retrospect," "Christianity in an atomic age," and "The threat of secularism," or reminiscent of lore as in "The shepherds, the scientists, and Simeon." Some titles are straight allegories such as "Nailing our colors to the mast," whilst others are topological such as "The divine overruling," "Dangerous silence," and "Protests." Some are argumentative as in "Citizens of two kingdoms," "Victorious faith conquering prejudice," and "The rightful claims of Heaven and Earth," whilst others are explicative as in "Race tensions in South Africa," "Modern madness and the cure of Christ," and "The world Church and human need."

The start of the sermon is crucial, to shake the congregation from their sleep. Most of the sermons start with a biblical text: some with one quote as in "Modern madness and the cure of Christ" or "Resolutions," others with two quotes, as in "Citizens of two kingdoms"—both from the New Testament—or "Christianity and the atomic age"—both from the Old Testament—or in "Absolute loyalty," from both the New and the Old Testaments. Rarely do we have three initial biblical quotes as in "The shepherds, the scientists and Simeon," featuring two quotes from Luke and one from Matthew. Most are from the four Gospels, from Acts of the Apostles, and the epistles of St. Paul; others are borrowed from Exodus, the book of Daniel, 2 Kings, Zechariah, and the Psalms. The text is often repeated within the sermon, as rhetorical and pedagogical device, etching the message into the heart and memory of the audience.

An expository sermon may start with a definition or terminology. This is the case for "Dangerous silence" and "The threat of secularism," explaining the connotation of the word "silence" and the definition and denotation of "secularism."

Topological exegesis often starts with an exhortation: St. Paul telling Timothy to preach incessantly in "Harvest Festival," or with a striking narrative like Quiller-Couch's experience as a boy of a "fire and brimstone" sermon in "Eternal life: Heaven and hell," which brings about the question of the place of judgment within the forgiving Christian Church.

Topology and anagoge are often mixed as in "Let my people go," with Moses demanding of Pharaoh to let the Jews leave Egypt and the Council of Churches urgent preaching against Hitler, anti-Semitism, and the Holocaust. Anagogical sermons may start with a striking narrative: the collapse of the Peru bridge in "The divine overruling," or a metaphoric description of reality—the determination to overcome death and to promote life—as in "*Resurgam*": this inscription of sheer determination is carved on the stone in the new-planted geranium garden growing out of the rubble caused by the German raid, in Plymouth, England.

Poetry and literary quotes may set the tone at the start. John Keats's serves as a foil at the beginning of "The realism of the Gospel," whilst the Scot, Robert Burns's, at the beginning of "The perils of our calling," introduces the notion of self-knowledge attained, "warts and all," through the mirror of others.

Rarely do we have an allusion to personal life, as in "The rightful claims of Heaven and Earth," where the minister, apologetically, alludes to his sadness at leaving South Africa, and preaches a sort of testament to his fellowmen and "beloved country."

The ends of sermons also vary in technique; some conclude on a warm and consoling note; others aim to move the heart to thoughtful action.

"The divine overruling" belongs to the first category; attempts at restoring calm and faith to the bruised members mourning the death of their children in the London School comes through the mouth of a child, reminding her benevolent but saturnine father of the amazing beauty and wonders of the God-created world. In "Absolute Loyalty" the final point of overcoming death with the love and presence of Christ is brought home by the story of the soldier who died in peace because his faithful comrade came back to hear his last words.

Faithful to the Word, Davies often ends his sermons with biblical quotes. Two biblical quotes on the comfort of the "presence" of a suffering Christ mark the end of "Absolute loyalty." Final biblical quotes abound in "The persistence of goodness in an evil world," with the goal to comfort and reassure. "Christianity in an atomic age" diffuses anger by a quote from the Council of Churches calling for patience and wisdom in the face of the sempiternal need to overcome historical challenges.

Encouragement and *caveat* recur at the end of "Race-tensions in South Africa" in terms of visual chiaroscuro: "The total situation, especially to those in the thick of it, may seem depressingly crepuscular, but light increases in intensity in this dark sub-Continent." In contrast, "Modern madness and the cure of Christ" ends on an auditory cry of longing for the return of Christ to all who are sick and heavy laden, with Thomas Lynch's poem, *O where is he that trod the sea?* A minister and son of a doctor—he had eventually become incapacitated.

An invalid might search the sky, but valid citizens should be stirred to action. This is the theme of nudging sermons.

In "The realism of the Gospel," Davies focuses his light on past and present apathy—omissions—by altering one word of a poem to apply the message to his congregation and shame them into political action: "When Jesus came to Wallington (instead of Birmingham), they simply passed him by." "A victorious faith conquering prejudice" starts with a biblical text enjoining the sharing of wealth, and ends on a prayer for awareness:

Lord, in the hour of tumult,
Lord, in the night of fears;
Keep open, oh keep open,
My eyes, my ears!

Not blindly, not in hatred;
Lord, let me do my part;
Keep open, oh, keep open,
My mind, my heart.

In England, many sermons end on an urgent request for action on behalf of the Jews and the persecuted. "Let my people go" and "The realism of the Gospel" argue that Christianity needs to be systematic in its demand for human rights. "The world Church and human need" insists on the duty of the voting citizen. The point is repeated to the young graduates of Lehigh University in "Protests, profound and trivial."

Davies can be more pressing, using rhetoric: apostrophe and exclamation marks punctuate "Nailing our colors to the mast." We hear the injunction: "Then in God's name, nail your colors to the mast! Live for Christ and speak up for Christ!" The message is softened in "Retrospect" as: "My beloved people, if we have that gift in our eyes, let us proclaim it simply, urgently, incessantly." To the quest for righteous action "No apologies" leaves the answer to four lines from *The whole garden will bow*, a hymn from the slave-trader, John Newton, whose conversion experience was similar to Paul's. Incidentally the hymn was put to music by Haydn, an Austrian and a Catholic. "Dangerous silence" ends on the words of repentance uttered by the sinned-against, but forgiving lepers, assuming responsibility, and warning the besieged king of the availability of food, left by his fleeing enemies.

So many different endings and yet the same theme. Davies appears here as a virtuoso.

Davies varies the speed of his endings, pulling out all the stops of the organ, or letting the still small voice of silence speak. The end of "Citizens of two kingdoms," trumpets patriotic pride and fairness—"O, to be an Englishman," of "no mean city" to boot—whose duty is to resist Nazi domination, as did Paul against Roman tyranny. Davies finishes on a long period, with anaphora and repetitions of the initial text, contrasted with short final *pointe:*

> "I am a citizen of no mean city." So are we, citizens of no mean city, London. So are we citizens of no mean Empire: one that has been given a magnificent privilege in these days. But also—and this is our most priceless privilege—we are fellow-citizens with the saints and of the household of faith; we belong to that company which numbers all the people of God who lived by faith under the old Covenant, which includes all, in all nations who responded to the call of God in Christ, from the first fishermen to all fishers of men. We belong to the elect, the chosen of God who created us, who loved us and redeemed us and who now empowers us.
>
> To him alone be the glory, who has made us citizens of two kingdoms. Of his Kingdom there shall be no end.

A similar building up technique appears in "The modernity of the master," resting on chiasmus and antitheses, before the final thrust:

> We need not only the Gospel of Christ; we need the Christ of the Gospel. We need to trust in the truth; but it is so much more helpful to trust in Jesus, the truth of God made flesh. We rest not only in the Sermon on the Mount, but in the one who preached it and lived it. We cling not only to the words that will never pass away, but to the Christ who will never pass away.

Reducing his *pointe* to one sentence in "*Resurgam*," he answers the doomed gladiators' final words to Caesar: "We who are about to die, salute you," by the message of hope uttered by the soldiers of Christ: "We who are about to live, salute you." Assertion of faith in the survival of the Church also comes in one sentence at the end of "The threat of Secularism."

On a quiet note, poems or prayers in verse top some of the sermons to raise the spirit from earth to a vision of the eternal city. "The rightful claims of Heaven and Earth" ends on the vertical thrust of Wordsworth's *To a Skylark*. "The shepherds, the scientists and Simeon" praises the variety of talents who work in the vineyard of the Lord and asks Christ's blessing on all callings.

Finally some sermons finish on a simple bidding prayer, like Henry Alford's at the end of "Harvest festival." Thus end "Eternal Life: Heaven and Hell," "The Gospel and the reversal of human values," or "Hope against Hope."

THE USE OF HISTORY AND LITERATURE

As may be expected in sermons concerned with present woes, the minister had several ways of using ancient and modern history: to back up his allegations, console and prompt to action, link present history to the history of mankind, and oppose the accidents and mischiefs of history to the eternal way of life and salvation.

In "Race tensions in South Africa," a particularly touchy topic when Davies, who had already been under-fire in the blitz of London and peace-keeper among the troops for the YMCA in Germany, is coming as new founder of the religion department to the hot-bed of apartheid in South Africa, historical documents or speeches serve to back carefully his personal stand. Seven large extracts are quoted from historians, a bishop, a Dutch Commissary, the prime minister, and a liberal statesman.

To remind humanity both of its shame and its overcoming of human-created tragedy, "Absolute Loyalty" links, by analogy, some of the persecutions of the past, from Nebuchadnezzar, Antiochus Epiphanes, Domitian, and the martyrdom of Polycarp, to the ambitions of Hitler causing the bloodshed of the Battle of Britain and Arnhem. "The realism of the Gospel" names, as a warning, three rulers judged for their sins: Saul, David and Pilate.

"Let my people go" and "Nailing our Colors to the Mast" recall the flight of the Jews from Egypt and the tribulations of the North African Martyr, Perpetua. "The modernity of the master" alludes to the taking over by the Saracens in the eight century, the present cruel fight in the Balkans of Turks and Greeks, and the final rendition of Napoleon, whose overwhelming ambition was brought down by allied forces.

On the other side is the expression of respect for those visionary rulers or citizens who did not accept the *status quo*: Elizabeth I and her admirals struggling against Spain ("*Resurgam*"), the energetic Louis XIV, constantly working for the betterment of France ("No apology") and even Napoleon, the organizer, who finally realized that order could not be imposed on people without their consent ("Christianity in an Atomic Age").

Among the modern reformers Davies has respect for Spinoza, Keir Hardy, R. Moffat, Ludlow, Maurice, Kingsley, Karl Mannheim, and even Karl Marx, who, like St. Paul, but in a variety of ways, tried to bring progress in the world. Davies expresses also his admiration for scientists:

Pascal, Pasteur, C. Maxwell, Kelvin, and Sir James Jeans in "The shepherds, the scientists and Simeon." He refers to Lillian Adam Smith, Julian Huxley and Waddington in "Nailing our colors to the mast," and praises even the invention of atomic energy, despite his indignation at the mass-murder of Nagasaki.

Sadly enough, Davies reminds Christians in "The rightful claims of Heaven and Earth," that the history of the Church from Genghis Khan onwards often mirrors secular history: Amos witnessed such storms ("Christ and individual need 2"). Davies expands by giving examples from patristic to more recent times: Paul, Luther and the Catholic Church ("Nailing our colors to the mast"), the Pilgrim Fathers ("*Resurgam*"), the creation of many different orders within the Catholic Church and dominations within the Protestant Church ("Christianity and individual need"). Yet difficulties were surmounted by those Christians, who had learned from history: St. Paul, Athanasius, Thomas à Kempis, St. Francis, Bunyan, Baxter, among others, and, in modern times, Ronald Knox, Hugh Martin, J. Leslie Newbegin, A. E. Whitman, Bonhoeffer, A. Gunner, H. H. Farmer, Niemöller who resisted the Nazis, and the contemporary ecumenical movement praised in "Citizens of two kingdoms," in which Davies, as a lover of peace and reconciliation, was particularly active.

Through his use of historical examples, Davies depicts a struggling humanity within and without the Church, attempting to link the past, its ups and downs and its renascences, to the dark side of the present times, stirring both protest and hope.

Literature is used to the same effect. Besides Scripture which pervades all the text, we find some of Davies's favorite authors: Ben Johnson and Shakespeare in "The Modernity of the Master"; Bernard Shaw, H. G. Wells, Bunyan, Pascal, M. Roberts, Dorothy Sayers, Charles Williams, and T. S. Eliot in "The shepherds, the scientists and Simeon"; Angus Watson, Pepys, and G. K. Chesterton in "Nailing our colors to the mast"; Evelyn Waugh and Dr. Johnson in "The rightful claims of Heaven and Earth"; also Keats and Wordsworth, Milton and George MacDonald, among others.

Long quotes or summaries from literature serve either as illustration or exemplars. In "Dangerous Silence" the sermon starts with a synopsis of the beginning of Thornton Wilder's *The Bridge of San Luis Rey*. Taking on an omniscient perspective, Davies thus enters both into the mind of his counterpart, the bewildered priest, and into the minds and hearts of his grieving congregation. Both struggle on the side of the hill and seek answers, as Job did.

Yet at other times, Davies is not afraid of certainty, attacking the defects of clergy or his flock and, through the negative, lets his audience perceive his own stand. "Retrospect" is a straight exposition of his ministry's doubts and beliefs. But quotes from those writers who saw the Church go awry are mainly used for satirical purpose. In "The perils of our calling," extracts from Sinclair Lewis, *Elmer Gantry*, and Peter de Vries, *Mackerel Plaza*, serve to illustrate the woes of ministerial self-exaltation and excessive modernism, who pander to the appearance of the "plant" and themselves rather than serve the people forming the Body of Christ.

Turning to the minister's flock, he also uses narrative and literature to attack snobbery. He does so scathingly in "Victorious faith conquering prejudice," through evocation: the life stories of the Colonel's lady and Judy O' Grady, both from the same Catholic Church, have little common ground. In "Nailing our colors to the mast," the quote from Angus Watson's *My life* serves to deflate both racism and snobbery in a New York Presbyterian Church.

And yet American literature also provides him with the model he seeks: two ministers, one an open-minded and cultured Christian, the other an ascetic as in James Gould Cozzens's novel, *Men and Brethren*.

More gently, he riles at the children, old and young, of various congregations. Fascination for the preacher for wrong motive is illustrated by Bernanos, *The Diary of the Country Priest*, where children play a trick, flattering the priest's looks and neglecting his words; the narrative of the lady preacher in the Congo whose glasses, rather than her message, kept her audience intrigued, in "Harvest Festival," serves the same point.

Yet that "the child is father to the man," as Wordsworth puts it, also appears in two sermons. Davies uses Graham Greene's *Brighton Rock* to illustrate the ambiguity and reluctance of Christians to fully adhere to Christ's Way: the boy argues for delay to enjoy the fruits of the earth; to his *Carpe diem* the girl opposes *Memento mori* and the fear of the impending Last Judgment. Wisdom, in "The divine overruling," is probably not extracted from literature, but comes out of the mouth of the wondering child, smitten by the beauty and love of God's world. Was it apocrypha or drawn from the preacher's own life? Maybe. It is poetry in any case, and recalls Christ's particular affection for children.

LOGIC

Davies's sermons may have the appearance of ease, but underlying the appeal is some down-to-earth construction and logic.

"No apologies" responds to defeatism after Hiroshima. Its construction is straightforward. A topological sermon, the first sentence states shortly its topic: "Our faith is a fighting faith." After a reminder of the struggles of the leader, St. Paul, come the three parts of the sermon: 1. the equality of all men in front of God, including monarchs; 2. the primacy of the Gospel over human institutions; 3. the need for courage in the time of distress, for resisting greed after deprivation, and for expressing one's political creed.

Some sermons are circular: "Retrospect" deals with the concerns of the minister and congregation; it starts with alleged shortcomings of the minister, possible suggestions of the congregation, and continues on an affirmation of the minister's vision of how best he can serve God and his flock. The end returns to humility and the promise to try harder during the coming year.

"The rightful claims of Heaven and Earth" is cross-shaped: it covers the issues of the vertical and horizontal needs of life that stretch human beings on the cross. After surveying the history of the Church and of Christian civilization, it calls for a new commitment to social justice.

"The modernity of the Master" is composed in three parts based each on parallelism between the large—History—and the small—personal history. It starts with a list of personal tragedies, leading to consolation and an appeal to courage: no use crying, the preacher says, be flexible, you will overcome. There follows an example from history: the hardships caused by the Napoleonic blockade gave birth to four Societies concerned with social issues. Davies then addresses the feeling of insignificance and answers it by the Testaments' promise to and alliance with the chosen people needed to proclaim the Word and the Way. And last, responding to the feeling of insecurity of his parishioners, he recalls man's irrationality that led to the Cross and the least glamorous parts of the history of Christianity. But they were overcome at the Resurrection.

"*Resurgam*'s" construction is still more complex, a sermon in the "modern" fashion. It starts with a narrative, then an apostrophe to the audience; it uses history to link three continents; its three points are the destruction of war, hope for peace in the presence of Christ, and the assurance that death is only a tunnel that leads to the Resurrection. It gives a final emotional example of a Canadian soldier, who, despite seeing one of his friends blown to pieces, affirms his faith: "It'll take more than that to stop God." After a final injunction, the sermon ends on an exhortation for peace in unity in South Africa.

"Let my people go" works its way through logic to counterbalance emotional bias and prejudice, to end eventually on the visualization of horrors to spur emotional and moral indignation. It first states three historical reasons for anti-Semitism: religious, historical, and economic/sociological. On the other side of the scale, Davies loads the achievement of the Jews from Moses's religious insight, philosophers, doctors and inventors, to artistic talents and politicians and argues against ingratitude on the part of Christians who, besides, have forgotten the very roots of their religion. The final thrust is a heart-rending quote from a Polish witness, Victor Golancz, depicting raw the cruelties imposed on the Jews, and thus arguing for protest against the German demon.

"Race tensions in South Africa" is also carefully crafted, to dedemonize, this time. Starting with a shock sentence of accusation against the Whites, Davies shows the complexity of the situation in South Africa: demographic, historical, economical, political and social. He then proceeds to examine three preferred solutions: assimilation, segregation or Christian trusteeship and ends on a high note of hope for the future to be achieved by the combination of politics, the Church, and education. The logic of the talk is meant to calm the heated spirit of well-intended but simplistic well-wishers.

An ecumenist and a lover of peace after having witnessed the ravages of war and of civil war, Davies always looks for balance: physical, intellectual and religious in "Christ and individual need," for instance, and social in "The Shepherds, the scientists and Simeon." He calls for equilibrium between the rights of heaven and the rights of the earth.

DELIVERY AND RHETORIC.

This desire for fairness and balance, what others might have called moderatism, which increased with maturity, was neither translated in the pulpit, where Davies preached with passion, nor in the style of his sermons: his use of History and Literature as examples, and careful Logic to advance the cause, vouch for that.

For balance in phraseology one reads in "The right claims of Heaven and Earth": "God should enable us to be on our guard against winning heaven at the cost of losing the loveliness of earth and the claims of social justice."

Because of the necessity of direct speech and direct message in times of crisis there are very few, if any, substitution figures like metonymies, synecdoche and periphrases, but images abound. We also find very few litotes or euphemisms, since persuasion often leads to amplification by use of anaphora and gradation.

Auditory elements like alliterations or assonances occur many times, as in "Christ and individual need 2": "His first supporters actually pawned clocks and dinner cutlery, and crockery to borrow money" and in "Nailing our colors to the mast," we hear that the minister of *Mackerel Plaza* effected "an impudent and impertinent change" on the biblical text.

As in Baptist preaching, the best of which Davies admired, repetitions serve rhythm and persuasion: repetitions of the same point, of the same phrase, and/or of the same biblical text. They are numerous in "Resolutions," "Retrospect," and "Christianity in the atomic age." In "Retrospect" the word "burden" is repeated four times, to be laid at the foot of the Cross. In "Resolutions," it is the word "vows." "The modernity of the master" insists on the opposition between the world and Christianity by using synonyms: "The world is mad, stark, staring, and raving mad."

A similar effect is created by anaphora. In "Christianity in the Atomic age," it stresses the guilt and need for reparation after Hiroshima and Nagasaki:

> No wonder the conscience of the Christian world has been scandalized by it. No wonder that the Roman Catholic Father Ronald Knox declares in his essay, "God and the Atom," that the use of the bomb on Hiroshima without preliminary harmless warning demonstration of its power has lowered our self-respect. No wonder either, that many churchmen in the United States are already planning a campaign for funds to rebuild these cities as costly acts of self-imposed reparation.

In "Retrospect," repetition is combined with apostrophe and rhetorical questioning, to shake the congregation out of torpor:

> What are your thoughts in the pew? Do you sometimes think what your minister's thoughts must be? Do you ever think that he

shudders when he rises on a cold and wet morning, knowing that because of the weather, many that Sunday are going to leave God out in the cold and stay at home fire-watching? Do you ever think, when he is absent from the pulpit, that in the other church where he is preaching, he hopes against hope that you will show your steadfastness to Christ by attending? Do you ever know ...?

And in "The realism of the Gospel," irony is added for the sake of persuasion: "You who purr about the earthly beauty of Christ; you who cuddle up to the comfort of God, realize the Savior of life came not to bring peace but the sword."

Short and terse are some antitheses, paradoxes and chiasmus which emphasize the logic of being a Christian or the illogicality of life. One reads in "Modern madness..." about the lunatic: "No man could any more bind him with a chain. Because he had been often bound with fetters and chain." Attacking the use of weapons of mass destruction, Davies says: "We had a military conquest, but a moral defeat." Chiasmus abound in "Nailing our colors to the mast" and we read in "The modernity of the Master": "We need not only the Gospel of Christ; we need the Christ of the Gospel."

Davies plays the chromatic scale: the black of "indiscriminate bombing of Coventry and London and Plymouth and Hull and Southampton," topped by "the blackest deed in all history"; the dark grey and gruesome red of the horrors of the concentration camps; the lighter grey and fast pace of man's demands from bread to television, whilst forgetting his soul's need, in "Christianity and individual need 1"; and the pinky grey frou-frou needs of the Colonel's lady of "Victorious faith conquering prejudice."

Humor releases the tension. It is rarer in the sermons addressed to a world in crisis than, for instance, in "Monarch of Men," but it still appears: the vows that we do not intend to keep; the story of the confused chameleon, which, put on a Scottish plaid, turns to grey; the satire of the Puritans," wearing their hats "that looked like church steeples"; and the depiction of the academic, Dr. Marshall, "the greatest living authority on the private life of the ferret." In "Monarch of men: Jesus man of prayer" we find the flippant remark:

> We parade our doubts in a kind of religious Ascot; the newer the fashion of the doubt, the more we are to be admired. Can you conceive of one woman saying to another: "You've only got arthritis,

but I've rheumatism in every limb. What do you think of that? That's something to be proud of?"

In *Believing*, we saw that Davies turned to colloquialism to address the man of the pub; in America, he uses it to speak to the youth. In "Hoping against hope" we hear about the despair of a humanity orphaned from God, with the comment: "and what is left but to whistle in the dark to keep one's spirits up?" or on the present disregard for Christianity, that people have abandoned "Christian hope and written it off as mere dreaming, sheer fantasy in cloud-cuckoo-land."

Finally sermons strike the imagination through bold imagery. The audience will remember "The realism of the Gospel" for its auctioneer who roared like a bulldog but was only an ostrich, for the depiction of the Church as mere air-shelter and the Gospel as "warm bath or cold shower, chloroform and tonic." In "Harvest Festival" they will remember the trodden path as a patchwork quilt, the thorny path crowded by golf and tennis, and the chameleon on the stony soil. Images abound, from nature, the daily life of agriculture and shopkeeping, the military and seafaring life, from sickness and health, both in body and mind, added to the usual Christian symbolism of the cradle, the gallows, and the tomb. In "Monarch of men: Jesus baptized" they will envision John's followers as "children in the marketplace playing at funerals, whereas Jesus's wanted to dance."

Sin-weary and saddened by this heart-breaking world, Davies did not preach the Kingdom "as if it were the cigarette-ends of our life," but with hard work and a "coruscating" culture and imagination, nourished by years of historical and literary studies. He, like Ariel of *A Midsummer's night dream*, spreads the drops of vocabulary, logic, history, literature, rhetoric, and imagery to redress the sins and foibles of men, deliver them from despair and coax them on the right path. In short, this volume of sermons is not the dull reflection of "a burnt out cinder" but "a flame of fire" using technique and intelligence to light up "flame[s] of fire burning for his kingdom."

1

The Perils of Our Calling

*An Oxford Sermon Illustrated from
Contemporary Literature*

IT WAS A MAN and a poet who had suffered much from the inquisitorial ministers of the eighteenth century established Church of Scotland, Robert Burns, who cried:

> O wad some Pow'rr the giftie gie us
> To see oursels as ithers see us!
> It wad frae mony a blunder free us,
> An' foolish notion.

Ministers, more than the rest of men, because of their high calling in Christ Jesus, need such mirrors, quite apart from that transcendent image of the ministry, who was pre-eminently the icon or mirror of the invisible God, our blessed Lord himself. But where are they to be found? In our wives? But the mirror is misted over with affection when the lady of the manse looks at the minister (or one hopes it is.) Would our congregations provide a truer reflection? Even her distortion is likelier than true reflection. For the admirers of the minister hold out the golden mirror of adulation, in which he is, being human, only too ready to recognize the idealized image of himself. And the critics of his congregation either steel silently away to another congregation, or so enrage him with their exaggerations, that what he sees in the mirror is the image of a misunderstood martyr to the truth, haloed in righteous indignation.

That is why I believe our novelists, whether sympathetic or satirical, can perform the service of enabling us to see ourselves as others see us. To be sure, there will be distortions as well as reflections in their representations, but the very distortions will serve to point out the peculiar perils of our calling, whether they be pomposity, petulance, complacency, conventionalism, snobbishness, triteness, and, above all, conformity to the world in its social values and groveling worship of success. The novelist is singularly adept in baring the hypocrisies that take those and myriad other protean forms.

The criticisms will also be counterbalanced by sympathetic portraits of the ministry. These will serve as encouragements in a profession which receives many tokens of affection, but aptly not the highest in a materialistic world. Such portrayals will be inducements to the life of charity in a world of cheap sarcasms and character-assassination; they will stimulate that forgiveness that mends embittered relationships; they will help to increase that compassion which always runs the second mile in helpfulness, and that openness which looks for the best in every human being, recognizing, beneath the rust and dust of the coin, the divine image which our Lord came to restore to our soiled humanity; and they will encourage that steady submission to the rule of God with the assistance of Divine Grace that brings direction and a holy content to our frantic and bewildered moderns.

I want to point to three peculiar temptations of the ministry in our own era, as these are pinpointed in the novelists.

1. The vulgar and sentimental cult of *peddling the parson's personality*, which, as it was Apollos's defect in the Corinthian Church, produces the same disturbing effect today of attaching a congregation to a man, not to the Lord of the Church and its Head, our Savior.

The most heinous example of such a type, in modern literature is, of course, Sinclair Lewis's *Elmer Gantry*, which should be required reading in all Reformed and Evangelical Theological Colleges. Here is the epitaph of a Baptist minister and Evangelist who believed, contrary to St. Paul, that the minister's motto is: "We preach ourselves, not Christ crucified." It is also a most discriminating analysis of the skin-deep pietist culture in which Gantry was brought up: pragmatism instead of revelation's authority, sentimentalism without the transforming ethical obedience of faith. It is a brave warning against a merely muscular Christianity, a hail-fellow-well-met religion. Elmer Gantry has only two native abilities: a gift of the gab and the complete equipment of the extrovert—a roaring voice and a backslapping manner. Says Lewis: "He was born to be a Senator. He never said anything important, and he always said it sonorously. He could make 'Good Morning' seem as profound as Kant, welcoming as a brass-band, and uplifting as a cathedral organ."

Yet the fault was that religion was taught to him as a series of melodramatic possibilities and sentimentalities. In Sunday School, he learned the story of little lame Tom who shamed the wicked rich man who owned the team of grays; and of the faithful dog who saved his master from a fire, and thus roused him to give up one trinity of delights—horse-racing, rum and the harmonica—for the Holy Trinity. Lewis shows that his conversion is simply the result of crowd-psychology in which the President of the Theological College pleads in an orgy of emotionalism for this Very Important Young Man to enter the Kingdom. No wonder he thought he was conferring an honor on the ministry!

At the theological seminary, he picked up confidence in elocution, an impressive vocabulary, and a pretentious smattering of learned languages. His only honor was to win a ten-dollar prize in practical theology for an essay on "Thirteen ways of paying a church debt." We shall not follow his career of personality-pushing to its sorry and inevitable conclusion, except to reflect on his great success as minister of "The Wellspring Methodist Church in Zenith, Winnemac." Its moral is that catering to sensationalism leads to more exaggerated sensationalism. It ends in titillation, not truth.

These temptations may attract us in a much more subtle way, in proportion to our training and Christian culture, subtler than Elmer's. It will most likely take the form of commending the Gospel for its by-products rather than its truth—that is the shape of modern theological pragmatism. We may commend the faith because of its comfort-value, not its radical soul-surgery. We may commend it because of the moral security it will offer, when faith is the commitment to insecurity; we may commend the Gospel for mental health or public morale or as an escape-hatch from the racial and social problems of the day. And we may only commend ourselves.

2. *Dazzling men without cultural achievements.* The second peril of our Calling, especially if we have been privileged to study in Oxford and to nurture our Christian thought and devotion in such a college as Mansfield, is the temptation to dazzle men without cultural achievements—to be ambassadors of Parnassus, not of Christ—to be, in a word, intellectual snobs. The temptation of culture-pandering is peculiarly strong in Communions that appreciate a learned ministry, especially in

suburban areas. It has been most brilliantly exposed in Peter de Vries's book *The Mackerel Plaza*.

In the Reverend Mr. Mackerel's spotty scale of values aesthetics come first, and culture a close second. As might be expected, he wishes to be thought anything but a minister of the Gospel. Meeting a well-rounded municipal secretary, she says, in surprise: "Oh, you're the ...?" She recoiled a step in surprise, then laughed and said apologitically. "But you're too young. You can't be more than thirty-five. And you certainly don't look like a preacher." De Vries comments on Mackerel's response: "This pleased Mackerel. Mackerel so disliked the term preacher, and so abhorred the term brother as a designation for the clergy that he was always grateful for their inapplicability to himself. The most insidious temptations he ever faced was the wish to run with The Hound of Heaven and the socialite and intellectual hounds of earth. The pomaded poodles he found quite irresistible."

Bernanos has shown the answer to the problem of unconsciously seeking popularity in the *Diary of a Country Priest*, when his country priest learns that the gravest danger of his calling is to hope for personal affection to him, for this is a failure to attach souls to Christ. He learns this, when he has completed a series of lessons on the catechism to the girls of the village and has just awarded Seraphita Dumouchel the weekly prize, whose pertness he mistakes for zealous piety. He asks her:

> "Aren't you longing to welcome our Lord Jesus Christ? Doesn't it seem a long time to wait for your first Communion?"
>
> "No," she answered, "why should it? It will come soon enough." I was non-plussed, but not generaly shocked, because I knew the malice there is in children. So I went on. "But you understand me, though. You listen so well." Her small face hardened and she stared: "It's cause you've got such lovely eyes."
>
> Naturally I didn't move a muscle, and we came out of the sacristy together. All the other children were outside whispering and they suddenly stopped and shouted with laughter. Obviously, they planned the joke together.

The priest learns that God is an enemy of easy speeches that comfort cruel men. He confesses: "When the Lord has drawn from me some word for the good of souls, I know, because of the pain of it."

He has learnt the bliss of Beatitude: "Blessed are ye when men persecute you and revile you and say all manner of evil against you for my sake ... for great shall be your reward in heaven."

Part One

Preaching During World War II

2

Citizens of Two Kingdoms

Preached in Wallington, during the Blitz of London

This sermon is an undisguised appeal for the defeat of Nazism and the invasion of Germany, despite the citizens' desire to be loyal both to the State and to God, on account of two arguments: Germany has flaunted both Human Rights in its persecution of the Jews and the Second Commandment against the worshipping of false idols, by installing the new Caesar, the Führer, as the Savior of mankind.

- Acts 21:39: "I am ... a Jew of Tarsus ... a citizen of no mean city."
- Ephesians 2:19: "But ye are fellow-citizens with the saints and of the household of God."

THE GREATEST OF THE apostles (but, in his own estimation the "least") was a citizen of two cities and a member of two kingdoms. He was a free-born citizen of Tarsus, claiming all the privileges of Roman protection. He was also a citizen of the kingdom of God, one of the members of the household of faith. When the early Church was in its infancy, there was no necessary clash between the two loyalties. But when Rome realized that the followers of the Lord could not bow to any other sovereignty, that they must serve him whose name is above every name, then persecution began. The issue was narrowed down to Christ-worship or Emperor-worship. The Book of Revelation is a moving record of the bitter conflict between the earthly Roman kingdom, claiming heavenly Lordship, and the saints, protesting that they were good citizens of Rome, because they were bound to a higher allegiance. In this, the final book of the Canon of the New Testament, the saints are shown dying for testimony to the Word made Flesh. "I saw underneath the altar the souls of them that had been slain for the Word of God and for the testimony they had held."

So it has been and is in our own day on the continent of Europe. Wherever the saints of the household of faith have declared their supreme loyalty unwaveringly, persecuting has followed. We recall only a few famous names out of a great number of fellow citizens with the saints. Pastor Niemöller in Germany, tortured beyond human endurance, was sustained only by the Lord God, whose unflinching witness he is. Bishop Berrgrav of Norway was then centre of Christian resistance, and the symbol of the claims of the kingdom of God in Norway "with God in the darkness." Protestants and Catholics throughout the continent of Europe have resisted the claims of a pagan government to dominate their life. Some have fallen away (but who are we to suggest that we should have survived the ordeal?); some have fallen asleep; some are even now sealing their testimonies to the Lord with their blood. They are those "of whom the world was not worthy." Their citizenship is in Heaven, because the earthly power claimed rights over their souls, which belong to God alone.

They were useful citizens of the earthly kingdom, until the rulers of the earthly kingdom demanded that they renounce their citizenship in the Kingdom of God. This fact forces upon us the question: are these loyalties exclusive? If one is to offer the supreme allegiance to the Kingdom of God, does that necessarily mean a repudiation of the earthly citizenship?

1. Where the State is the custodian of the law of nature, that is, where the rights and duties of men to worship God are safeguarded, the members of the Kingdom are in duty bound to support the State, which is appointed by God to preserve the society of men, who cohere in justice.

Often there will be tension. For the Church, in the name of God, we as citizens of God's kingdom, are necessarily the spokesmen of God against false standards, against social injustices. That is part of the prophethood of all believers: to remind the State that it is appointed by God to preserve the society of men. This was the truth so clearly perceived by the misnamed "social gospellers." We therefore take part in all the activities of citizenship, partly as a recognition that we have received innumerable benefits, under God, from the State; partly also, because through our Christian insights we are enabled by God to act as a "leaven" in society. But we do [it], most of all, to express our Christian conviction of "brotherliness." Where the State officially recognizes the Christian Faith, as in this country, the tension momentarily is relaxed.

2. But where the State claims divine powers, substitutes an earthly leader as the arbiter of destiny (as in Germany and as in Japan), where the State in fact repudiates the Kingdom of God, then we too "must obey God and not men." Think of that repudiation in terms of its significance in modern Germany, and you will give glory to God for those who have literally become martyrs for the Kingdom of God. Remember that and you must remember them in your prayers.

He who has ears to hear today knows what the Spirit of God is saying to the Churches: the central things of our faith have become central again. "In this world ye shall have tribulations" says our Lord, "but be of good cheer, I have overcome the world." Words of the very Word of God have been the very marrow of their resistance, the nourishment of their heroic souls, as they are ours.

God has given to the Christian leaders on the Continent a very profound insight into his will, and a deep sense of dependence upon him, when all earthly supports have fallen. That is why their words to us demand that we study afresh the Word of God which has miraculously sustained them in the day of trouble and they advise us to fight the ungodly tyranny of Nazism with physical and spiritual weapons, for two reasons. And these reasons were conveyed to Dr. Micklem when in the year of München, he paid a visit to the leaders of the Church resistance movement. As he left Germany, he said: "What advice am I to give to your Christian brethren in Britain?"

"Tell them," said the Protestants, "that the purity of the Gospel is endangered."

"Tell them," said the Catholics, "that the foundations of our Christian civilization are endangered."

Because the earthly kingdom claimed to dominate the Kingdom of God, the earthly kingdom itself was imperiled—we know it. Look at the treatment of the Jews; can we pretend that brotherliness is a recognized principle in German life? Consider the deliberate breaking up of homes in Germany, Holland and France, the deportation of all nationalities, and the utter fear that prevails in Germany; men have lost their natural human rights. By the deliberate Nazification of all teaching, there is—in no rhetorical sense—a veritable kingdom of lies, a domain of sin on the Continent. "Tell them that the foundations of Christian civilization are imperiled." Remember that the Churches have been taught to declare a Gospel which regards Adolf Hitler as the Savior of modern Germany, and *Mein Kampf,* as the Word of God. Remember this and you will know the truth of that advice: "Tell them that the purity of the Gospel is endangered."

In the interests of the earthly kingdom, which, under the hand of God, provides justice for mankind, the sooner we and our allies bring Nazism to its knees, the better for Germany, and the better for the rest of the world.

In the interests of the Church of Germany, now in secret cellars, in concentration camps, the sooner we invade Germany, the better.

But when all is said, the chief purpose of the Church is not simply to be the custodian of the rights and duties of mankind. Our task as Christians is to make the Church so dominant, so to declare the Gospel of the grace of God, that men, everywhere, in all nations, may be translated from the Kingdom of darkness into the Kingdom of the love of God's dear Son. To declare it, without fear or favor, to speak for it, to live it, that the new order may be laid upon the only foundation that is unshaken in these days—the foundation which is already laid in Jesus Christ. In his Church, the body of Christ, we belong to a kingdom which spans over empires and which contains in it the whole company of earth and heaven. It is because we belong to that glorious company that can serve the State and be above the State.

"I am a citizen of no mean city." So are we citizens of no mean city, London. So are we citizens of no mean Empire: one that has been given a magnificent privilege in these days. But also—and this is our most priceless privilege—we are fellow-citizens with the saints and of the household of faith; we belong to that company which numbers all the people of God who lived by faith under the old Covenant, which includes all, in all nations who responded to the call of God in Christ, from the first fishermen to all fishers of men. We belong to the elect, the chosen of God who created us, who loved us and redeemed us and who now empowers us.

To him alone be the glory, who has made us citizens of two kingdoms. Of his Kingdom there shall be no end.

3

Harvest Festival

Preached in Wallington, London
Sunday Evening, September 27, 1942

As the fruits of the earth are celebrated at the Harvest Festival, Christ rejoices in the crop of souls gathered in his Church; not the Church triumphant, however, but the Church grateful for the Sower of the Word. The sermon continues with an anagogical explanation of the Parable of the Sower—the parable of the "four soils." It ends on a note of hope that all souls' soil can be improved to receive the Word of God.

ST. PAUL, YOU WILL remember, from the Ordination service, exhorts Timothy to "Preach the Word: be ready in season, out of season." What word can one preach at the Harvest Festival? Surely, you say, here is an opportunity to thank God for the fruits of the earth and the seas and for the labor which tended them and disturbed them? Yes I agree. It is a time for gratitude but not for self-congratulation. Has not the Lord a deeper word for us? He has; for the earthly Harvest is but a symbol of the Divine Harvest of the in-gathering of souls. That is what I must offer you tonight.

Our Savior's own theme is my theme. The Parable of the Sower is what it is popularly called. It might be called, more to the point, the Parable of the Harvest; but its best title is "The parable of the four soils." In each case it was the same sower; in each case the same atmospheric and climactic conditions had their influence. But the soils were different.

Now a parable is like a problem picture or an ordinance survey map; before it is understood, it requires a key. The key to unlock this inner meaning of the story is a very simple one. The seed is the Word of God, the

Message of God; the sower is the Lord himself or his agents who preach the word. The soil is the human personality to whom it is preached. The four soils are, therefore, the four types of souls to whom God addresses his word. And the harvest is dependant upon the willing response of the soul to the preacher; as the harvest of the seeds is dependant upon the receptivity and fertility of the soil; for soil, read soul.

THE FOUR SOILS/SOULS

The Trodden Path

Some of the seeds fall on the trodden path. You know the narrow paths that cut across cornfields like the joining of a patch-work quilt. Or the other paths that run along the hedge sides. These paths were useful, but they would not grow corn. For all the result, the farmer might as well have sown the seeds on the stone floor of his farmhouse kitchen.

Do you know people like that? I do. We say of such obstinate folks: "You might as well talk to a brick wall" or "It fell off him like water from a duck's back." Such people (as the Greek word reminds us) simply do not take it in. They are impervious.

Perhaps Jesus was thinking of the closed minds of some of the Jewish religious teachers. Their minds were made up. How do they get like that?

They will not concentrate or make any efforts to understand. Hugh Martin tells us of a certain missionary who went to the Congo. She was amazed and thrilled by the undivided attention given her by a group of African women. They leaned forward eagerly and gazed at her wonderstruck. When she paused for a moment, one of the women asked her eagerly: "What are those glass things on your nose?" Their attention had never really got beyond her spectacles.

Some people's minds are worn smooth by the constant traffic of lazy thoughts and idle trifles. They are superficial; they live on the surface. They have no deep interests. They can't bear to sit still with a book for an hour. They would be bored by a serious conversation about anything. They must have something to pass the time, and very often all they can find in their leisure hours to do is to listen to maudlin crooning and syrupy sentimentality on the radio. Poor things, it is not always their own fault that they get like that, but it is a pathetically distressful situation.

Other people allow the spiritual sides of their natures to go hardened by neglect, so that they do not know that it is there. They are just not receptive to religious ideas. Religion is just irrelevant to them. There is nothing in them, so they think, that responds to it.

In war-time, we may easily fall in with their neglect. So many other demands upon our time, so much straining for the national effort, may suffocate and throttle the religious breath in us. We may well pray for them and for ourselves: "From all the hardness of heart and contempt of the Word and commandments, good Lord, deliver us."

The Stony Soil

Some seeds fell on stony soil. Now this was not, as one might imagine, a field strewn with small stones, but a thin layer of soil over solid rock. Such places are characteristic of large areas of Palestine, where the rock is near the surface. The same is true of our English Lake District. The point about this type of soil is that it is shallow soil.

The Galileans are said to have been like this shallow soil, an emotional, turbulent people, with quick but unstable enthusiasm. Shakespeare in one of his loveliest sonnets says: "Love is not love / which alters when it alteration finds." The Galileans were not a sturdy sacrificial race; they were always on the lookout for new interests and new enthusiasms. They altered when they found alterations . . . And not only the Galileans, but the Athenians also. The apostle Paul tells us that they were running after any new thing.

But such people can be found nearer home still. They are the first recruits of any fad in religion or politics or art. It takes them barely a moment to discover that this new point of view is the greatest discovery of all time. The Gospel according to Bernard Shaw is much more desirable than the good news that comes from Christ. To them the rights of man according to H. G. Wells carry more authority than the Ten Commandments. Even that expert in camouflage, the chameleon, cannot compete with the rapidity with which they respond to the color of their environment.

You find them in religious circles. They will welcome the new minister with enthusiasm, so long as he remains new. They are not insincere. They mean every word they say. It is all real as far as it goes, but it does not go too far. Their enthusiasms have not roots.

This surely must explain why Jesus at times seems almost to discourage people who wanted to follow him. "Lord I will follow Thee wheresoever thou goest." "Do you really mean it?" says Jesus. "Think what you are saying. It is no picnic, following me." "Foxes have holes and the birds in the air have nests. But the Son of Man hath not where to lay his head." (Luke 9:57–58)

The trouble is that a too-ready enthusiasm often means an over-readiness to yield to difficulty and persecution. Such people are susceptible to religion; but they are also susceptible to ridicule. A sneer or a joke is just as effective to them as the thumbscrew or the stake. They like to stand well with their fellows and they believe in doing in Rome as the Romans do. They will make a Christian Profession as long as there is no persecution or opposition. They have no roots.

They are Bunyan's character, Pliable. He was readily persuaded to go with Christian on his pilgrimage and he was delighted by his descriptions of the goal of the journey. What could be lovelier than the cherubim and seraphim, the golden crowns and golden harps and the ten-thousand of saints? But then the road came to the Slough of Despond and that didn't fit in with the description of the Celestial City. So he went away and Christian saw him no more. He returned to his neighbors in the City of Destruction and "sat sneaking among them ... and began to deride poor Christian behind his back."

The Thorny Soil

Some fell among thorns. The soil is excellent but other things were in occupation. You cannot grow two crops at once on the same part of the same field. You must choose between thorn and corn.

Men are so preoccupied with business and pleasure that they have little time for religion. Our Lord says that thorns may come from cares or riches or pleasure. The cares may be those of poverty. It is hard for the poor man to be a Christian. He is troubled about the future, perhaps even about the next meal. He is worried about the welfare of his wife and family. Our Savior sympathized and so must we.

But our Lord also taught that it may be even more difficult for a wealthy man to be a Christian. Great possessions and the love of money-making are at least as dangerous an enemy of high-thinking and noble living.

In truth, both riches and poverty, both luxury and want, suck the goodness out of the soil. There are different kinds of thorns, but they both choke the corn.

Many of us would have to confess that we were trying to grow two crops at once. We are Christians only in patches. Our lives need weeding badly. "Create in me a clean heart, O God."

The Good Soil

After all most of the soil is good normal soil. The crowning harvest makes the losses insignificant. Every farmer expects to lose seed. He knows that the birds will get some and that other seeds will not ripen. But he does not therefore despair of a good harvest.

Patience is required for the cultivation of the crops and for the cultivation of the soul. No man becomes a Christian all of a sudden. More patience is required than for the reduction of a golf handicap or the improvement of one's tennis strokes. But it is incomparably more worth while. Discouragements will come but, with God's help, we shall not give up trying until we become what Christ would have us be.

Perhaps no one parable tells all of the story. You may have been wondering: can the other three soils be changed? The parable does not. But this we know: the soil trodden down can be ploughed; the shallow soil can have other soil added to it; the thorns can be uprooted. Christ is Savior as well as Teacher, Ploughman as well as Sower.

If Christ awakens no response in our heart, whose fault is this? Is it the fault of religion, the seed or the fault of the preacher? Or perhaps, it is our own fault, the fault of the soil?

If this harvest service is to be real to you, kneel by your bedside tonight and utter T. Dudley-Smith's simple prayer: "Grant, O harvest Lord, that we / Wholesome grain and pure may be."

4

The Shepherds, the Scientists, and Simeon

Preached in Wallington, London
Advent, 1942

Three types of people recognized God in the child Jesus, sent away by the inn-keeper. Using historical convergence, Davies shows that they are a good sample of society. The shepherds adumbrate the workers, disaffected first with the Church, then with Marxism, who might respond to the social gospel. The Magi, seekers of wisdom—since Religion, Philosophy and Science were one in ancient times—are seen as the forebears, rich in knowledge and generosity, of the all too specialized and skeptical scientists of the modern age; they need the Church to broaden their outlook. Simeon and Anna represent the faithful, old and wise, both patient and impatient with history's misdemeanors. Still young at heart, they welcome the new generation with hope for betterment and renewal.

- Luke 2:8: "And there were in the same country shepherds abiding in the field, keeping watch over their flock by night."

- Matthew 2:1: "Now when Jesus was born in Bethlehem of Judaea in the days of Herod the king, behold, there came wise men from the east to Jerusalem."

- Luke 2:25: "And, behold, there was a man in Jerusalem whose name was Simeon, and the same man was just and devout, waiting for the consolation of Israel."

THE INN-KEEPERS AT BETHLEHEM resolutely bolted their doors as Joseph sought admittance for his wife and little one. It was a poor welcome for the Christ-child. But it would be wrong to say that no one greeted the Infant-Savior. Like the King he was, he had his heralds, although unexpected ones. In fact three sets of people brought him their greetings. The sentinels of the night—the shepherds of Bethlehem—hastened to the babe in the manger. The star-gazers of Chaldea were scanning the skies for signs of hope; and those who waited "for the consolation of Israel" were upon the watchtower in the temple at Jerusalem.

Our Savior was greeted by the shepherds, the scientists, and Simeon. Each of them represented a different class and type of mankind. Each of them received a different sign.

The shepherds represent the workers, the men who work with their hands. To them was given the most easily recognized sign: the angels' glory and the angels' song. It was a sign discernible to both eyes and ears, and unmistakable.

The wise men, the astrologers, who were the only scientists of the day, represent the students of the world: the observers and thinkers. To them was given a sign which could be seen by the eye but which required interpretation by the mind.

Thirdly, there was the devout, aged group in the Temple, the circle within a circle, the spiritually discerning in spirit. For them, there was no outward sign, simply an inward token, and a spiritual assurance. We shall look at each of the groups in turn.

THE SHEPHERDS

An unreal aura of glamour has been put over the heads of these shepherds particularly as Jesus pictured himself as the Good Shepherd. But the truth is that they were perfectly normal shepherds, doing their regular job. They were rough, muscular men, with gnarled hands, and probably spoke with a burr. And they were simple people with few opportunities of knowledge. That night we may presume that they were talking about the sheep and their prospects at the market, and their homes and children. There is no sign that they are seekers after a new revelation of God. John Milton pictures the common-place character of the scene:

> These shepherds on the lawn,
> Or ere the point of dawn,
> Sat simply chatting in a rustic row.
> Full little thought they then
> That the mighty Pan

> Was kindly come to live with them below.
> Perhaps their loves, or else their sheep,
> Was all that did their silly thoughts so busy keep.

They were ordinary people about their ordinary tasks. That is the amazing thing about spiritual blessedness. Its offer comes to men who are not seekers. Jesus emphasized this in the parable of the pearl of great price and in the hidden treasure. The pearl merchant had been searching for years, but the discovery of the hidden treasure just happened.

Jesus taught that great opportunities come to those who are not seekers. The Shepherds were of that company. They were humble, biddable, unsophisticated. They left their flocks and hurried to meet the child.

The Gospel of Christ has great kinship with the worker. The shepherds were the favored of the earth in receiving the first notification of the Savior's birth. Jesus chose his comrades from among fishermen, men of toil. There is nothing artificial about the normal life of the worker, no invitation to idleness or fastidiousness. He is honestly hungry and rightfully weary, helping to get the work of the world done. Such are the people to whom Christ can make his appeal.

Are the workers of this country divorced from religion today? The bitter truth is that they have tired of the patronage of the Churches and turned to a new Messiah, Karl Marx. I remember reading a poem by a working-class man which ended: "Stands the church blocking out the sun."

You know what the author meant: the complacency and the respectability of the Churches was a barrier between the working man and the Son of Righteousness. The vested interests of the Church stand as the barricade to the Christian freedom of the working man. Any Church that does not give a welcome to the worker, [nor] speaks to his heart, [nor] concerns itself about his welfare is deeply at fault. The first tidings of Christ's coming were given to workingmen. And remember that our Free Churches owe their spread to the artisan class and the merchants. O workers of England know that Jesus Christ is your word, the inspiration of social justice and sympathetic reform.

THE SCIENTISTS

Who were the Wise Men from the East? We know very little about them, except that they were students who were also seekers. They were men on the watch, scanning the skies and the records, inquiring for the truth of things. They were the investigators and philosophers of their times—the first-century scientists.

It is to be noticed that they were prepared to give new truth a hearing, even if it came in an unfamiliar way. They studied the stars but they were prepared to welcome a man who was a king. Their knowledge did not prevent enrichment through faith. And they had princely hearts: they brought costly gifts and did not hesitate to bestow their gifts at a lowly child's cradle.

What of today? Have the thinkers deserted the Church? Is it not a true accusation? Remember that Pascal and Pasteur, Clerk Maxwell and Kelvin all died in the Christian faith. And today Skepticism and Agnosticism are practically due for retirement. Our chief poet and essayist, T. S. Eliot, wrote a poem immediately after the last war, symptomatic of the generation, called *The Waste Land*, but since then he has entered the Promised Land and his second most famous poem is *The Rock*, the confession of Peter, the basis of the Christian Church.

I might mention other astute minds of our generation: Sir James Jeans who is a Christian, Michael Roberts, Dorothy Sayers, and Charles Williams, for instance. And, in this reversal of opinion, I quote Bernard Shaw: "It is a great relief to me to find that even the choice spirits among the college professors' literally God-forsaken lot, are ceasing to parrot obvious anti-clerical nonsense in the firm belief that they are teaching science." He adds that young people of today are not as puzzled as their fathers were by the fact that Sir Arthur Eddington, great as an astronomer, a professed friend of Shaw's, that Faraday and Darwin and Tyndall were members of religious sects.

The tide of unbelief is turning. What is the Church's message to the thinkers today? Not that they think too much but that their range of thought is too restricted. Their detailed knowledge of the constitution and of the laws of matter does not fit them to be judges of the operations of the mind. The scientist knows too much about too little. That was amusingly suggested when Manson presented Dr. Marshall for the honorary degree of Dr.-ès-Science at the University of Manchester, in these words: "I present to you a scientist who may be described briefly though not exhaustively as the greatest living authority on the private life of the ferret."

But that does not entitle him to speak authoritatively on the private devotional life of the Christian. The scientist needs to broaden his scope:

an expert in his own field, he must be a humble inquirer in the Christian field.

It was harder for the wise men to come than for the shepherds. They had a less obvious sign, a long journey, and a more difficult enquiry to make. But they brought more; the shepherds had to come empty-handed. The wise men brought rare and costly gifts of gold, frankincense, and myrrh. It is still the same. It is harder for the thinker to find Christ, but when he comes, he has more to bring.

THE THIRD GROUP: SIMEON AND ANNA

They were aged, deeply devout and had a special quality in their faith, Simeon and Anna were the elect of the nation—the church within the Church. They looked for the redemption of Jerusalem and waited for the consolation of Israel. God had whispered in their ear. They knew a great Deliverer was at hand. Other Jews were excited at the possibility of a Messiah. They knew.

One wonders: they were so old, yet they had an unconquerable hope. Their expectation came wholly from the unseen. Their whole life was prayer and yet more prayer. Removed from earth's toils and struggles, indeed, half in heaven already, they had developed a rare spiritual sensitivity.

They were able to recognize the expected One without a sign. There appeared before them a Jewish artisan and his wife, and a babe. George Mac Donald's poem says:

> They were all looking for a king
> To slay their foes and lift them high
> Thou cam'st a little baby thing,
> That made a woman cry!

No, not all were looking for a king. These two were not. Their hearts knew by the fire that leapt within that he was the Messiah. They needed neither star nor angel to find the Lord.

Their successors are still amongst us, these people with simple hearts, whose chief interest is God and his ways with men. They keep open the doors whereby God can communicate with men, help us to believe in the unseen, and give us spiritual courage. They are wise, very wise, with the wisdom of the child's heart and the matured mind. They cannot argue for their faith but the testimony of their lives is unimpeachable, and carries true conviction with it. Blessed is the Church which possesses such saints.

Today Jesus comes to the man of toil, the man of thought and the man of prayer. The toiler says: "I haven't time to investigate; and so much is uncertain." But Christ suits his tokens to his need. Where the heart is honest and wistful, he comes: deeper knowledge brings deeper trust. Will the toiler say: "Let us go now, even to Bethlehem"?

The thinker may say: "I cannot easily pray. I am staggered by the assertion that God became man. It is too great to be easily believed." But suppose that God became man so that searching might find certainty. Are your eyes towards the sky?

The natural Christian, who finds prayer a delight, must find an added welcome: "I have seen thy Salvation."

May our Lord hover around men of every type and task.

5

The Modernity of the Master

*Preached in Wallington, London
December 6, 1942*

This sermon is based on reflexions after conversations with parishioners, as the war is intensifying. To counter the sense of the hollowness of life and the endless repetition of historical tragedies, the preacher offers the new institutions that were created in awareness of the arising problems, and the enduring Church. Against the feeling of personal insignificance created by the mass-organization of modern society, he offers the people's active participation in God's plan. In response to the need for security and the awakened awareness of evil and the irrational in human beings, he offers the Cross and the imitation of the patience and faith of Christ.

- Hebrews 13:8: "Jesus Christ is the same yesterday, and today and forever."

- "He belongs to the after Lincoln/ As the curtain goes down on the final act of Abraham."

BEN JONSON SAID OF his fellow dramatist Shakespeare that he was not for an age but for all time. I want to make the same claim for Jesus Christ that his mission and his message are as relevant today as yesterday. And in a sense this sermon is not going to be preached by me but by you. Much of it is the fruit of visitation and conversation with you. This talk will be an attempt to show you that our Master has the answers to the questions you ask and the problems you want solved. It is an attempt to show you that your deepest needs are answered by him. That he speaks to our modern condition. See how he meets the needs of the life maladies.

Human Life Is Hollow and Meaningless

That is the first symptom of the malady of the age. It is very hard to prove this statement because people are good at disguising their feelings, at whistling in the dark. They may even put up a placard to the effect that they are not interested in the possibilities of defeat. But that is bravado. As Gilbert Murray said of an earlier age: "They had a failure of nerve."

During the last war a name was coined by French doctors for this disease of the spirit, which made its appearance in prison-camps. They called it barbed wire sickness. Its chief symptom is an appalling sense of the meaninglessness of life. No matter what camp-activities were organized, whether community-singing or dramatic performances, no matter what books were distributed, nothing could quite banish from the mind the awareness of the barbed-wire enclosure, the sense of standing-still and of sheer inanition.

The same is true of human spirit today. Life is closed on itself. This finds expression in many phrases: "It's all very well for you to talk of a new world; but it will be the same as the old. How can we go on hoping, we did that after the last war—the more fools we." Sometimes a man says: "What's the use?" he shrugs his shoulders and that's that. There is no denying the fact that war has so altered the plans of many that life does seem to have lost its purpose.

The businessman, after an honorable career as a trusted servant, prepares to retire, but has to go back to harder toil in his declining years.

The mother, who lost one of her sons in the last war, now sees the second, even though he is a married man, go out East.

The father, who has sacrificed to obtain his son a good education to set him on his feet, sees the son, his education incomplete, go into khaki ... And so it goes on. No wonder he asks whether the world will be any different.

There are only two responses to this depression: the escapist's and the realist's. The escapist drowns his sorrows in drink or buries his nose in novels or his mind in bridge. But the realist, thank God, determines to face the worst and build upon it the best. He seeks what Winifred Holtby calls a "constructive application" to every tragedy. If his business has crashed, he develops a new line. If his premises were blitzed, he takes temporary premises elsewhere. If his wife dies from cancer, he determines to spend what he has on cancer research. If his son goes to war, he will fight that his son may return to a worthier England.

It is this spirit that is supremely exhibited by the Christian faith. One hundred and fifty years ago this country was threatened by the invasion of Napoleon. A historian tells us: "Many doubted the endurance of our wooden walls and hearts of oak, and went to sleep half prepared to be aroused by tap of drum or glare of beacon-fire." Farmers brought back from market lengths of bunting to be run up their church-towers on the first news of the landing of the French. In great houses in Norfolk coaches were kept ready to whirl the women and children into the depths of the Fen country. There was justification for this for the government had issued "Regulations for the Preservation of Good Order, to be adopted in case of actual invasion." Arrangements had been made for the safety of Queen Charlotte and the royal princesses; an armed escort was ready with thirty wagons to bury the treasure of the Bank of England in the crypt of Worcester Cathedral. Futility reigned; people refused to discuss post-war problems. Yet the very times that tried men's souls moved them to good purpose. The escapists bolted, the realists planned.

Yet during these years in which the war with Napoleon raged, in 1792, the Baptist Missionary Society was founded, when transport was almost impossible; three years later, in 1795, the L.M.S. was founded; a year later, 1796, saw the inception of for the society for Bettering the Condition of the Poor; when the terror was at its height, seven years later, in 1803, the Sunday School union was founded and the British and Foreign Bible Society. When England was besieged, the missionary movements contemplated the Christian invasion of the continent.

In this war-divided world, the only bridges left between the nations are the Christian Churches. Man's littleness becomes great when linked to the chain of God. Empires set, politicians rise and fall, governments are in and out of office, and moods of triumph are succeeded by moods of despair. But the Church of God goes enduring on. In the spirit of Christ we are more than conquerors; earthly set-backs are the clarions of the Kingdom of God. I say to you men and women, God's champions: the very despair of our times makes Christ relevant more than ever; it makes men with a purpose, and clean hands a veritable necessity. Man's extremity is God's opportunity and ours.

Allied to Despair in the Modern Mind Is a Sense of Man's Personal Insignificance

A. Gunner in the R. A. recently expressed this in the following lines of a poem:

> Why should I dance the dance of death,
> While my mad spirit gives me breath?
> A man of no identity,
> I wear a mask;
> It fits me for convention's task.

To use the current psychological jargon we all suffer from an inferiority complex. Sooner or later you catch every one you know defending or asserting his own importance. There is so much touchiness and readiness to take offence that people are all the time fighting against a sense of personal insignificance. Galsworthy says rightly that the strongest motives determining human behavior are not those which spring from the instincts and impulses which men share with the brutes, such as sex and hunger, but those which spring from his desire to "save face." And the most exaggerated nationalism of modern times has sprung from a country where there was more inferiority feeling per square head than anywhere else in the world.

This is in part the result of the mass-organization of modern society and the widespread depersonalization of modern industry. Man is simply an unimportant cog in a machine. If he is sick or retires, the management can easily replace him. It is also the result of our class divisions, values and honors, which stimulates the desires of many but can only please the few.

Here is where Jesus Christ meets the need of modern insignificant man, takes him out of the context of machinery, where he does not count as a mere employee, and invites him to become a partner in the greatest enterprise the world has ever known—the winning over of men.

There is a devil as well as a hero in the soul; as there is horror as well as hope in the cross. "Be of good cheer," says the Savior, "I have overcome the world." That is the secret of the triumphant adequacy of Christ.

He, by his life and death and resurrection has the very things that modern men cry out for. Is your life futile? Plan with Christ the conquest of the world and know that God wins every one of his battles: he sits secure upon the throne of the universe.

Do you feel insignificant, of no account? Then remember you are a recruit of the army of God, sworn to root out evil in politics and in business. God has commissioned you for the world's biggest task: the making of new men. Do you feel insecure? Then rest on the promises of God in Jesus Christ. "Lo, I am with you even to the end of the world." "In my Father's House, there are many mansions." These are securities of more than gilt-edged value.

Our confidence is in him who abides faithful, even though we change, as Martin Luther put it:

> A safe stronghold our God is still;
> A trusty shield and weapon . . .
> And though they take our life
> Goods, honor, children, wife,
> Yet is their profit small;
> These things shall vanish all
> The city of God remaineth.

Jesus Christ is able to give a man a sense of balance. It rids him of his egoism as it abases him before the cross; and gives him meaning and confidence as he is included within the scope of God's plan.

Thirdly, Modern Man Yearns for a Sense of Security.

He does not altogether desire safety first. He longs for adventure; but he wants a stable background. Just as the explorer will only risk his own life if he knows his wife and family will be cared for. As Dr. H. H. Farmer reminds us: "There is adventure in being at sea in a seaworthy boat with storm rising; there is no adventure in being at sea in such circumstances in a sieve."

Those who have been in an earthquake tell of the ghastliness of the feeling of all inclusive insecurity. It is a feeling like that which shatters the confidence of modern man, the sense that the whole framework of life is rocking and shifting. When we are in exalted mood we say: "Mankind has struck its tents and is on the march again." On a less ecstatic plane we say: "everything is in the melting pot." When we have the uncomfortable sense of foreboding, we say: "Civilization seems to be collapsing and God alone knows what will rise from the ruins."

And this belief is shown in a shocked and frightened awareness of the forces of evil and unreason which are at work in history. The fate of the Jews in the Polish ghettoes can only be called diabolic, as well as the children in Greece and occupied Europe dying by their hundreds. It is the fact that evil can be so successful and even calculatingly sought after that terrifies people.

What has our Savior to say to this? He simply says that to look at his Cross is to show the unreason and madness of men, all that was diabolical conspired to put the Son of God upon the jagged tree. There evil appears at its most devilish. But there also, the invincibility of goodness is shown. The shame of the entire world is the hope of the entire world.

It happened when the Saracen hammered at the gates of hope and men said Christendom is lost; it happened at the Reformation, when the Church was more like the widow of Christ than his Bride. It happened at the Methodist revival, when a dying Church heard on its deathbed the call "Arise, O Zion, for the Lord is come." It is going to happen again. The signs can already be seen in many a church, where the chosen of Christ are bearing on their bodies and their souls the marks of the Lord Jesus —men and women literally broken and spent in suffering compassion for the world.

Heaven and earth pass away, our Lord never. Do you remember St Francis and how the miracle of the resurrection happened for him? When all the gilded splendor of St. Peter's Rome, proud, ornate, boasted its wealth, he met a beggar, exacting only a crust or a few coins and his outraged soul reflected: the Church cannot say "Silver and gold have I none"; therefore she cannot say "In the name of Jesus Christ of Nazareth, rise up and walk." If the Church takes up the name of Jesus and does not obey his Commandments, it is dead, a gilded corpse. The time of the resurrection of Christendom is always when the Church listens to the voice of Christ and obeys it, and amid all the uncertainties of human guidance, it accepts the ringing challenge and the sturdy comfort of the risen Son of God.

If we were asked what the bedrock of our faith is, we should answer: "Faith in Christ." But there is something even deeper than that: Christ's confidence in himself. There are times when our faith wavers, and when like the warrior on the field of Edgehill we say: "I shall be busy this day," or "I may forget thee, do not thou forget me." We stand most firmly not on our faith in Christ, but in the Lord's faith in himself. In one sad hour our Savior doubted the fidelity of man: "When the Son of man cometh, shall he find faith on earth?" But his faith in the Gospel of the love of God never faltered or fainted. There was a black moment on Calvary when the cry of a deserted soul broke from his lips. It seemed awful to the innocent one of God that truth should stand upon the scaffold, but he did not doubt that it was truth that stood there. In the agony of our Savior the destroying fear that he was dying for a fiction never entered his soul. To the judgment bar of Pilate, with malicious priests and an angered crowd outside, and cowardly judge before him, he does not hesitate: "To this end was I born and for this cause came I into the world that I might bear witness to the truth."

I cannot exaggerate the steadies that this conviction that the confidence of Christ brings to us in the spiritual struggle. It heals, it fortifies, it inspires.

When our own faith falters we fall back on the faith of Christ. When in the heat of the battle panic creeps upon our spirits, and men about us are crying that all is lost, we lift our faces to the General of our salvation and the world's and reassure ourselves with the victory in his eye. We need not only the Gospel of Christ; we need the Christ of the Gospel. We need to trust in the truth; but it is so much more helpful to trust in Jesus, the truth of God made flesh. We rest not only in the Sermon on the Mount, but in the one who preached it and lived it. We cling not only to the words that will never pass away, but to the Christ who will never pass away. We respond to his invitation "Believe in me." Christ's confidence in himself is the ground of our confidence. We would believe in him, that God pities us. That is the abiding comfort of the Gospel: it is not only love, but love incarnate. And the challenge and unspeakable privilege of the Gospel is that it lives on in the world through "living epistles," not in printed words, but in obedient hearts and lives and actions that are the Gospel and bring the assurance of faith to human tragedy, the love of God to human need, and the hands of Christ to heal.

6

Absolute Loyalty

Preached in Wallington, London

Harassment and torture, deprivation of earthly goods and the penalty of death have always been the means by which tyranny curbs dissent. Here, provided by Daniel's dire experience under Antiochus Epiphanes, is a recounting and an explanation of the story of the three youths in the fiery furnace, who refused to recant their faith, went through trial, and found Jesus walking out of the ordeal with them. With examples from past Roman, Jewish, and Christian history, this buoying story of heroism and loyalty is applied to current history.

- Matthew 10:24–40: [Love God and do not fear]

- Daniel 3:17–18: "Our God whom we serve is able to deliver us from the burning fiery furnace, and he will deliver us out of thine hand, O King. But if not, be it known unto Thee, O King, that we will not serve thy gods, nor worship the golden image which Thou hast set up."

THE BOOK OF DANIEL, like the Book of Revelation, comes out of great tribulation. It was born in a crisis. A foreign dictator, Antiochus Epiphanes, was trying to force a pagan religion down the throats of the Jews. His methods have been followed by Hitler in Germany. He began by deposing the rightful High-Priest and placing a puppet in his place. He then declared all Jewish practices illegal. Sabbath observance, worship and sacrifice were forbidden; even the sacred Scriptures were burned. Then came the last straw. He entered the Holy of Holies in the Jewish Temple and there set up an image of the Greek god Zeus, and burned swine upon it. The Jews could not tolerate this bitter insult to their religion and they rose to arms, the whole nation like one man. After a murderous struggle they shook off the pagan tyranny.

The book of Daniel was written during the war to encourage men and women to be loyal to their faith in God, whatever the cost. Its known author recalls the stories of brave men in the history of the Jews, who faced a cruel death rather than deny their God.

The contemplation of past heroism breeds new heroes. In the same way no doubt in the far future when England's life may be at stake, men and women will read with proud eyes the exploits of the brave few who won the Battle of Britain in the skies, or of those gallant men who walked through the burning hail of steel to Arnhem.

CRUEL CHOICE

Here then is the story of three youths who are forced to make a cruel choice. Either they must fall down before the golden image of Babylon, the symbol of that totalitarian regime, or they face not banishment or loss of their goods or imprisonment, but death by being burnt alive. There were two alternatives: disloyalty or death, apostasy or martyrdom.

This story portrays a choice that is typical in Christian history. The early Christians in Rome had to offer sacrifice to an image of the emperor, or go to the stake. If a man would not consent to sprinkle a few grains of incense on the imperial, he was thrown into the arena to be torn limb from limb by the ravenous lions. "Curse Christ and be free" urged the magistrate in Smyrna, when Polycarp was arraigned by the mob. "Eighty and six years have I served him." Replied the venerable bishop "and he never did me wrong. How then shall I curse my King who saved me?" He and the noble army of martyrs chose death rather than yield to Caesar what belonged only to God.

Today the Confessional Church in Germany is faced with the same cruel choice. The State has claimed divine honors; Hitler has usurped the place of God. For those who refuse to bow down to the swastika, there is reserved the lingering death of the concentration camp.

COURAGEOUS REPLY

Now look at the reply of those youths. They say two things:

1. They affirm the omnipotence of God: "Our God, whom we serve, is able to deliver us out of the burning fiery furnace."

The God whom we serve is the supreme governor of heaven and earth and all power belongs to him. He does not share his sovereignty with any other. There is no division of his Kingdom. Even the devil, as once Luther asserted, is God's devil. It was, you will remember, when the Church was thrown into the Domitian fires of persecution that the Book of Revelation was written. And, in that book, the omnipotence of God is affirmed "King of kings and Lord of lords. And he shall reign for ever and ever." The Hallelujah chorus was first sung above the roaring of the flames of persecution, and the blood-curdling shrieks of the tortured. The expiring Christ, on whom the world had spent its murderous blows, cried "Into thy hands, O Father, I commend my soul."

2. The brave three also pledge their unconditional loyalty to God. God could, if he wished, rescue them from their fate. But, even if he did not, they would not deny him. "Our God whom we serve is able . . . But if not, we will not serve thy gods . . . nor worship the golden image thou hast set up."

These men do not serve God for what they can get. They do not stop to bargain or haggle with him. Their loyalty is without conditions and without hesitations. Happy is the man who can say, as Job did, with his provocations: "Though He slay me, yet will I trust Him." This, and nothing less, is what the Christian faith demands. Our Lord calls for an allegiance that supersedes all earthly relationships: "He that loveth father or mother more than Me, is not worthy of Me: He that loveth son or daughter more than Me is not worthy of Me." And, "He that taketh not his cross and followeth after Me is not worthy of Me." "He that findeth his life shall lose it: and he that loseth his life for my sake shall find it."

RESULT

What was the result of this courageous stand? What happened to those three youths?

Well, God did not deliver them: there was no miraculous intervention: bound hand and foot they had to face the ordeal by fire. But they came through it unharmed. They were not delivered, but they were preserved.

Then Nebuchadnezzar, the king, was astonished. And rose up in haste and spoke, and said unto his counselors: "Did we not cast three men into the midst of the fire?" They answered and said unto the king "True, O King." He said "Lo, I see four men loose, walking in the midst of the fire and they have no hurt. And the form of the fourth is like the Son of God." He saw they were unharmed by the fire because God himself came down and passed through it with them. In all their afflictions he was afflicted. Because he was there they discovered the truth of the words of the prophet: "When thou walkest through the fire, thou shalt not be burned; neither shall the flame kindle upon thee."

Christ did not promise his followers immunity from affliction, or escape from trouble. On the contrary he promised blood and toil and tears and sweat. "Ye shall be hated of all men for my sake." "I came not to send peace, but a sword." "Blessed are ye when men shall revile you and persecute you and say all manner of evil against you falsely for my sake." But we are not to pass through the burning, fiery furnace alone. He says: "Lo, I am with you always, even unto the end of the world."

During the Great War, a soldier asked permission to rescue his friend who was lying severely wounded, a casualty in no-man's-land. His officer consented, but reluctantly. The wounded man was probably dead, he pointed out, and the would-be rescuer ran the risk of losing his own life. But the soldier was not to be dissuaded. He wriggled out of the trench, crawled to where his comrade lay and managed to drag him back. But he himself was fatally injured in the attempt. The two men finally tumbled into the trench and lay silent in the mud. "There," said the officer, "I told you it wouldn't be worth it. Your friend is dead and you are mortally wounded." "Yes, sir," he gasped, "but it was worth it because, when I got to him, he said 'I knew you'd come.'"

"Yea though I walk through the valley of the shadow of death, I will fear no evil: for Thou art with me."

"In the world, ye shall have tribulation," says our Lord, "but be of good cheer; I have overcome the world."

7

Let My People Go

Preached in Wallington, London
Sunday, March 21, 1943

This exhortation and call to action examines the historical, sociological and psychological causes of anti-Semitism, its disastrous consequences, and the cures that committed Christians can bring about through the democratic process.

I TAKE AS MY text the words of Moses to King Pharaoh, the tyrant: "Let my people go." They are famous because they mark the beginning of what we have known as the "Jewish Problem." This is my theme this afternoon.

I am conscious that this is a very controversial issue and that it frequently rouses high feelings in the disputants. But I am not going to use this pulpit as a coward's castle. It is a Christian duty to think fearlessly and to speak fearlessly. It is also his duty to speak and think fairly. I shall be glad if I have been able to give your consciences guidance on a matter of urgent importance.

WHY ARE THE JEWS UNPOPULAR?

1. One very strong historical reason is that Christendom has always been suspicious of the race that put our Savior to death. For centuries every Christian child has been told that the answer to the question "Who killed Jesus Christ?" is "The Jews."

Today Christians would be the first to point out that it owes everything to a Jew, its founder in whose life, death and resurrection it finds salvation. A Christian would also point out that the early missionary activities of the Christian Church as well as the form of its organization, owes everything to another Jew, St. Paul.

This criticism is not a very vocal one these days, but its importance in days gone by has produced some of the features for which we dislike Jews. I maintain that the persecution of the Jews by the Christians of the Middle Ages has made the Jewish people into a Jewish problem.

Jewish persecution took two forms:

First, Jews were isolated. Jews and Christians had to be kept apart for fear that the Jews might convert Christians to their faith. In each town, a special street, or courtyard, was set aside for the exclusive use of the Jews. Gates were put up at each end of the Jewish street and Christian warders were stationed at each entrance. These were closed every evening as the angelus rang and remained shut until sunrise. By this isolation, intermarriage was forbidden and the Jews were forced to emphasize their own differences from other nations.

More than this, Pope Innocent III ordered that all unbelievers were to wear a distinctive badge to mark them off from all so-called "decent" Christians.

Already we are within sight of the German treatment of the Jews today. They are herded in ghettoes and forced to wear a badge of shame.

These very measures have produced in the Jews a strong national consciousness and an aloofness from other people. What we call the superiority and clannishness of the Jews are directly due to their treatment at the hands of the mediaeval Christian leaders and rulers.

Second, Jews are also unpopular. It is counted an offence that they engaged in money-lending, peddling, and the selling of second-hand articles.

Why did they concentrate on these activities? Because Christian Europe would not allow them to make their living in another way. No Jew could take any part in the government of his day, lest he should be in a position to rule, by his inferior administration, those who were "racially superior" to him.

Utterly excluded from the upper class of his day, he might seek employment in the guilds of craftsmen. But this was impossible since the guilds were religious confraternities, usually dedicated to a patron saint. If a Jew sought to work on the land as a serf, even that was impossible. For all the workers on the land had to take an oath of fealty to their overlord in the name of the Trinity. Thus peddling from town to town, usury and selling second-hand articles were the only occupations left to a Jew. Their lowliness only increased the disrespect felt by the Jews.

That Jews should have become infamous for driving hard bargains is not surprising, considering the hard hearts of their persecutors and the desperate struggle they had to exist. What Darwin described in the animal world as the "survival of the fittest," is a description that applies to the Jews. Their very qualities—sound business [sense] and ruthlessness, cunning and rapacity—are the result of the environment into which our Christian forebears pushed them.

Third, by a curious inconsistency, we dislike the Jews because of the eminent position many of them hold in the professions of today.

A hundred years ago, they were despised for a seemingly exclusive concern with commerce. When they were given opportunities for entering the professions, hitherto closed, we again raised our hands in alarm.

These charges are the main reason for the unpopularity of the Jews. But with them goes a large dose of ignorance, prejudice and German propaganda. The very distinctiveness of Jewish surnames accounts for much of this. If we read in the newspapers that some one has been convicted of a black-market offence, and his name is Thomas Smith, it evokes no comment from us. But if his name is Goldberg or Rubenstein, we murmur: "The Jews again."

I am not denying that there are two kinds of Jews: the good and the bad. All I am saying is that by their very names, the bad Jews are more prominently before our minds than the bad Englishmen because of their characteristic names. And I am also claiming that we Christians, who in the past treated the Jews like animals, are reaping in the cunning and acquisitiveness of the Jews, what we deserve: "We sowed the wind and we are reaping the whirlwind."

REMEDIES TO COMBAT ANTI-SEMITIC PREJUDICE

I find that the best remedies to combat my prejudice of the Jews are three.

1. First I recall what we owe to the Jews. To them as a nation we owe the deep insight into the character of God which is enshrined in the Old Testament, which is itself the cradle of Jesus Christ.

To individual Jews we are indebted in many ways. I remember that the whole outlook of our modern world has been transformed by three

Jews: Bergson's theory of Creative Evolution, Einstein's theory of Relativity and Freud's discovery of the Unconscious and of the new science of psychoanalysis. They have revolutionized our thinking.

I think of the contribution to modern health made by Ehrlich who discovered solvers; the effective antidote to venereal disease of Wasserman, whose reaction, named after him, enables the disease to be quickly identified. I think of Traube who discovered digitalis, used in severe cases of heart-disease; of Koller who discovered cocaine; of Minowsky who discovered the importance of insulin for diabetic patients.

I remember the contributions of Mendelssohn, Meyerbeer and Mahler to music, of Heine to poetry, of Proust to the novel, of André Maurois to biography and of Epstein to sculpture.

In England, I remember that we had two distinguished politicians in Disraeli and in the Marquis of Reading. I remember too that Dr. Banardo, who was of Jewish descent, established the world's greatest orphanage. Put all these benefits to mankind in the scale of your prejudice [against] the Jews.

2. The most valuable antidote of all is to remember that our blessed Savior was born and bred in a Jewish home. He had Jewish disciples, wept over Jerusalem and loved the common Jewish people. His servant Paul declared: "There is neither Jew, nor Greek . . . but all are one in Christ." In him all divisions of race are utterly abolished.

But we must do much more for the Jews than reflect on their achievements. Today Jew persecution is more cruelly acute than it has ever been in the history of the world. Stories of their suffering are now being repeated that would overrun the imagination, so horrible are they. A note issued by the Polish government in Great Britain informs us that of the three million Jews who were in Poland at the beginning of the war, over a million have died already. But let us, for a moment, forget statistics and remember that these are persons.

I am going to close with a quotation from Victor Golancz's pamphlet "Let my people go." He says:

> For a brief moment, be just one of these human beings, whose body, with its nerves can suffer so, with its mind and soul, with all its resources of terror and despair . . . ? Be the mother flinging her baby from a sixth-story window; be a girl of nine, torn from her parents and standing in the dark of a moving truck with two

corpses pressed closely to her; be an old Jew at the door of the electrocution chamber . . . You will then say, you will surely say: "What can I do?"

The detailed answer to this question is found in the rest of the pamphlet. But in short, it means that the responsibility rests upon you to write to your M.P., to the Home Secretary, the Foreign Secretary, to the local people, or to join the resolution urging that we and the Allied Nations should work out a plan of rescue and give the refugees the utmost facilities for safety.

The Jews today have no divinely prepared exit in a Red Sea that shall intervene between them and the Germans. Their exit depends not upon miracle but upon plans and sacrifice and above all upon our compassion. Here is something practical that we can do.

"In as much as you did unto the least of those my brethren, ye did it unto me."

8

The Persistance of Goodness in an Evil World

Sermon Notes; Preached in Wallington, London, November or December, 1944

These sermon notes emphasize the role of men and women who chose to serve God rather than the gods of money, security and fame, the first through service to the world and the second through the heroism of daily life. Finally, we may all reach a high point in heroism, at some stage inf our lives.

- Joshua 24:15: "Choose you this day whom ye will serve; whether the gods which your fathers served that were on the other side of the flood, or the gods of the Amorites, in whose land ye dwell; but as for me and my house, we will serve the Lord."

SOMETIMES IT SEEMS AS if the world is in the grip of false gods, Mars, Mercury, Venus, Midas, Lares, and Penates, and the Christian has to say like Joshua: "As for me and my house we will serve the Lord."

When faith burns low, I like to array before me certain beliefs that life has burned into me, guiding lights in the darkness of doubt. If you like, they are lighthouses with a steady beam amid the rooks and storms of life.

THE PERSISTENCE OF GOODNESS IN AN EVIL WORLD

In a world in which it does not pay to be good, what keeps men clinging bravely and obstinately to a good life? The mystery of goodness is a greater wonder than the mystery of evil. "Great is the mystery of godliness," says Paul. Many who might have had a "good time" turned their backs. Yet they never regretted it. Is that true of the ungodly?

For instance, James Chalmers before his martyrdom in New Guinea said: "Give me back these 21 years, standing daily in danger of death, with the savages ready with their spears to pin me to the ground or with their clubs to fell me to earth; give it me all back again and I will be your Missionary."

Another example is Scots's student, whose professor had marked him out for high distinction. At end of his course, he offered him the chair of Greek in an Australian university at £600 per year. The student thanked him warmly but gave reasons for refusal. The professor amazed replied: "Will you reject an offer like this to become a Cameroonian minister at £80 a year?" This student was J. P. Struthers, editor of *Morning Watch*.

Contemplating the sacrificial few, my own dim life receives a mighty impetus to faith. The road is not uncharted but beaten hard by the footsteps of the saints.

CHRISTIAN HEROES OF THE COMMON LIFE

A second lighthouse is the lives of men and women I have known as Christian heroes of the common life.

Their lives tried to the uttermost by the hardships of life can be explained by only one certainty—that God was in them—as in the vicarious suffering of a wife on behalf of a husband which partakes of his, the just for the unjust.

J. R. Seely speaks for us all in *Ecce Homo* in witnessing to the inspiration of the winsome goodness of lives we have known:

> Probably no one will deny that in Christian countries this higher-toned goodness, which we call holiness, has existed. Few will maintain that it has been exceedingly rare, perhaps the truth is that there has scarcely been a town in any Christian country since the time of Christ where a century has paused without exhibiting a character of such elevation that his mere presence has shamed the bad and made the good better, and has been felt at times like the presence of Almighty God. And, if this is so, has Christ failed? Or, can Christ die?

I BELIEVE IN GOD, AS MOST OF US DO IN THE END, BECAUSE WE HAVE THE WITNESS IN OURSELVES

Browning speaks of faith as a curtain hanging securely from certain points, but drooping every now and again into folds. We all have our high points of Christian experience. I think for instance of Shaftsbury at Eton, seeing the pauper's funeral, or Lincoln seeing a whipped slave. Our own experience has high points, like my first communion.

"As for me and my house, we will serve the Lord our God."

9

Modern Madness and the Cure of Christ

Preached in Wallington, London, February 11, 1945

This psychological sermon examines causes of modern insanity in historical and religious perspective. After accepting the notion of demon possession as a reality recognized world-wide, it identifies three main causes for the problem: the fear of death, the division between ethics and power, and the division of the individual into many different people wearing different hats in order to secure "success," rather than wholeness. It suggests that Christ is the cure with his call to service, freely given, although, for those who follow him, because of jealousy, crucifixion might ensue.

⁕ Mark 5:1–20: "The parable of the man with the unclean spirit."

IF WE ARE TO understand this mighty work of the Messiah restoring a lunatic to sanity, we must, for the time being, dismiss all modern explanations of lunacy from our minds. This story comes from a thought-world where insanity is not explained as physically conditioned or mentally caused. You will not find lunacy explained in terms of a lesion of the brain or of a tumor on the brain. Nor will you find it explained as due to mental obsessions or unconscious conflicts, or in terms of dissociation of personality. The Jews of the first century AD were not concerned with the immediate causes of insanity, physical or mental. They were concerned with ultimate causes: why insanity should exist in a world created by a righteous God. Quite simply, they attributed insanity and many other forms of diseases to the malignant powers of demons. It was believed that there existed a host of invisible evil beings who could control or possess human beings. To the early Christians their activity took many forms: they were the gods of heathen idolatry, they were the cause of the moral degeneration of pagan life and they were the enemies of Christ and his Church.

One of the great triumphs of Christ was his victory over them. Each new believer counted it as a precious possession in that, in the custodianship of Christ, he was delivered from the diabolical power of demons.

We need not be surprised, therefore, that the Gospels record many instances of demon-possession. St. Luke, the physician, takes demon-possession as a matter of course: he no more questions it than he questions the facts of disease.

One further explanation is also needed. With the belief in demons, there also existed the belief in exorcism. It was believed that demons could be expelled by the use of the proper means by the proper person. For the ordinary exorcist, the knowledge of the demon's name and the use of a formula were essential. Here, let me add that the modern psychological practice of suggestion is a proof that exorcism can be used with very great success. Sufferers from delusions are extremely suggestible. When there is belief in demons, when both the patient and the exorcist believe in the fact of possession and the power of the exorcist and when the exorcist exerts a hypnotic influence, invoking the aid of the Divine spirit to conquer evil, cures have taken place.

The modern world is disinclined to believe this set of beliefs. Against such dogmatism I want to place question marks: 1. In any view of the universe, it is unlikely that man is the only spiritual product of the universe; 2. the experience of educated European missionaries in heathen countries today leads them to go back to the belief that demon-possession is the only fact that will explain the life of their heathen neighbors (Miss Constance Fairhall and Papua); 3. the lack of evidence for demon-possession in Christian countries may be explained by their acceptance of the Christian faith and the operation of the Spirit. The triumph of Christ over the demons would produce exactly this result.

This is certain: that our Lord believed in demon-possession and that he regarded it as a proof of his Divine power. He said: "If I by the finger of God cast out demons, then is the Kingdom of God come among you."

Now for the story and its meaning today. It has two parts: each of them applicable to modern men and women.

THE DISEASE AND THE CURE

1. Consider the patient, and his disease. I want you to look at the significant details of this story. Every vivid touch is crammed with meaning.

"A man with an unclean spirit, who had his dwelling among the tombs." Here was a man obsessed with the fear of death. He lived in a cemetery, this ancient lunatic and modern men shake hands here. Both of them are terrified of death. Our civilization is so terrified of death, that the word is not mentioned in polite society. We find less agonizing names for death: "passing on" or "passing over" or "sleeping." Our ancestors who believed in the resurrection could afford to be realistic and carve a grinning skull on their tombstones, because they could write under it "O grave where is thy sting, O death where is thy victory?" But our civilization, which has banished Christ, must also banish all thought of death. In America, this is symbolized by the great Memorial Park called Forest Lawn. Every suggestion of gloom has been rigorously excluded from these Los Angeles precincts. The proprietors have been trying for years to find a smiling portrait of Christ to grace this graveyard, but none can be found. It is beautiful, but is it Christian? Such escapism does not tally with the Cross.

We cannot afford to smile in this country over our transatlantic neighbors. Isn't a cremation service our equivalent? Soft lights and sweet music dispel the shades and rose-trees and lily-ponds in the grounds. Yes, we are terrified of death. We live among the tombs: the pathetic crosses of Flanders, the hasty massed-burials in open trenches of today.

Look again at this lunatic and see the symptoms of our insanity.

2. No man could any more bind him with a chain. "Because he had been often bound with fetters and chain . . . and no man had strength to tame him."

Modern man has broken the chains and fetters that bound him. Our whole civilization was kept in bounds by the ten commandments; they were the standards of duty, the moral law kept under Jews, Moslems and Christians for 1,600 years or more. Individual trespassers there often were, but society was united in enforcing the responsibilities of men to one another.

In our time the strong men have burst their chains and shattered their fetters and whole nations have followed them into the realm of power-politics and aggression. Japan proclaims a sacred right for stealing China. Italy declares that it is her sacred destiny to appropriate Abyssinia. Germany declares that "Lebensraum," legitimate expansion, entitles her to subjugate her neighbors. Grey might easily have said: not the lights in

Europe are going out but the fetters and chains of Europe are bursting one by one.

By the mercy of God, the chains in England and America held. But many in both countries had broken their individual chains with the cry: every man for himself and the devil take the hindmost. No wonder an author taking the war as his theme, entitles his book *Insanity Fair*. The world is mad, stark, staring, and raving mad.

3. Look at another detail. When asked his name, the lunatic said: "My name is Legion." He was a thousand different people.

His was a divided, distracted life. There was a civil war going on inside him.

Are we not also in the same state? With St. Paul we cry: "I am in a strait between the two: having the desire to depart from and to be with Christ." Do we not cry with St. Augustine: "Oh Lord, make me chaste, but not yet"? Our name is Legion: we worship God, yes, but we worship success. We would love our neighbor as ourselves; but we will knock every breath of out of his body in business. One moment we are all for loyalty and love; another we are as rapacious and greedy as wolves. Divided, distracted men and women, how we long for a unifying loyalty in life, that will integrate our life!

That is our situation: like the demon-possessed man, we are driven to crying out with sorrow because we are tortured by the fears of death, we are tortured by the sheer devilry of men out of control, and because we are ourselves a legion of different persons. That is the diagnosis.

CHRIST IS THE CURE

I will not insult you by suggesting that what we need is a more determined effort to right ourselves, a kind of Cueism, a technique that will encourage us to say each day: "I'm getting better and better in every way." I heard of one member of a church, who had attended it for ten years under the same ministry, who one morning said to his friend: "I must leave. I get no help here. For the last ten years I have heard the same appeal couched in different words. All my minister is saying is this: 'Pull up your socks.' There's no Gospel in that."

What we need is not a pat on the back. We are men and women who have tried for years to put ourselves right. I tell you, our humanitarian efforts are useless, the blind are leading the blind; one sick man is attending another. Then why do we not turn to the Good Physician? Because his cure is too drastic and his remedy too revolutionary. "Men must needs love the highest when they see it." So the optimistic poet said. It is a lie. They crucified it. Today, the Germans dare not look upon the goodness of a Christ-filled man. They hide him in concentration-camps; they tortured, they bullied, and they used every means in their power to crush the soul of Pastor Niemöller. The sight of holiness is annihilating to the natural pagan man.

So it was at first to this poor lunatic. When he saw the rectitude of Christs it was the mirror for his own deformity. He cried out: "What have I to do with Thee, Jesus. Thou Son of the Most High God, I adjure Thee, by God, torment me not."

Your dissatisfaction with life, your divided impulses, the fears to which you are a prey, cry out for the absolute control of the Son of God. That is the only possible remedy. You must become the prisoner of Christ, the slave of the Son of God.

He, the risen Christ, will banish all fear from your heart; for He has walked through the valley of the shadow of death alone, and now He walks through that darkness with you. He goes to prepare a place for you. He, the risen Christ by his holy love will bind you, fetter and chain you, and in his service, you will find perfect freedom. He, the ever living Christ, will give you the dominating loyalty that your life needs:

> O where is he that trod the sea,
> O where is he that spake;
> And demons from their victims flee,
> The dead their slumbers break . . .
>
> O where is he that trod the sea,
> My soul, the Lord is here:
> Let all thy fears be hushed in thee;
> To leap, to look, to hear,
>
> Be thine: thy needs will satisfy.
> Art thou diseased or dumb,
> Or dost thou in thine hunger cry?
> "I come," saith Christ, "I come."

—T. T. Lynch, 1855

10

Nailing Our Colors to the Mast

A Lenten Sermon, preached in Clifftown, Southend-on-Sea on December 1944 in Berkshire, Wallington Congregational and Baptist Church in 1946; Westminster Row, Birmingham, September 16, 1946; Sutton Coldford Church, September 9, 1946

Evangelism requires that Christians be no chameleons, nor lukewarm followers of Christ with their minds distracted by the ever-changing discoveries of science, their souls by the snobbery and racism invading some Churches, or their lives by hardship and the fear of death, as if the Cross and the Resurrection had never been. The final buoyant message is to live life to the full, in the service of God and neighbor, proclaiming the Word of Christ.

- Romans 12:2: "And be not conformed to this world: but be ye transformed by the renewing of your mind, that ye may prove what is the good, and acceptable, and perfect will of God."

"Be ye not conformed to this world," says St Paul. His words ring out a relevant challenge to us today. We are not to be, like the Church of Laodicea, "neither hot nor cold," an ineffectual, tepid people. "Nail your colors to the mast," says St. Paul. "You are Christ's, and Christ is God's. Let the world see to whom you belong."

This word is first of all a warning not to be chameleons—lizards that change their colors with their surroundings, perpetually camouflaging themselves. Lilian Adam Smith, in her recent biography of her husband, tells of how she met her first chameleon. It was during a tour of Palestine. She writes:

> On our way down to Beirut by the tortuous mountain road, we stopped at a wayside khan. I noticed a strange black excrescence on the black head of the innkeeper; he saw my wondering look, came to the door of our vehicle and to my horror, picked the black lump from his head and laid it on my knee. I was wearing a straw-colored cotton dress and in a short space of time a lump of the same color was resting upon it. It was a chameleon.

It then became the companion of their journey. One day they lost it in their hotel. After prolonged searching, they found it hiding at the top of a dark green curtain. Its color was, of course, dark green. "We said," she writes, "we might have paid our way across Europe by showing him off, now grey against George's grey suit, now black against his boots, or brown upon our rug." Apparently the chameleon was only once unable to take on the color of its environment. A science master from Harrow school suggested that they put the lizard on a multicolored Scottish tartan plaid. The poor creature turned a dull sort of grey.

That is all very well for a weak animal to take on the colors of its surroundings as a protective measure, so that it shall be invisible to its foes. But it will not do for Christians. We are forbidden to take on the colors of the environment: "Be ye not conformed to this world, but be ye transformed..."

We are created in the image of God. That is where we differ from the animals who only obey their instincts. We are given freedom and that involves the responsibility to rise above the environment and to be renewed in our minds. Chameleons may change as their background changes, but Christians have to change their backgrounds.

We belong to a great tradition in Churchmanship. Today we call ourselves a Free Church. But our ancestors gloried in the names of Protestants and Nonconformists. They were separated from the world; indeed they were at war with the world as soldiers of Christ. "Be ye not conformed" was their battle-cry. Today, instead of the Church invading the world in the name of Christ, the world has invaded the Church.

The cry of the complacent and the lazy—the jelly-fish in the churches—is "keep abreast of the times." "Cut your cloth according to your coat." "Conform." How our great forefathers would have disowned us if they heard this cowardly talk of retrenchment.

Only this week, I came across a paragraph in the diary of Samuel Pepys, which showed how he failed to understand the conviction and moral strength of the Puritan Nonconformists. On August 7, 1664, he writes: "While we were talking, came by several poor creatures carried by constables, for being at a conventicler ... I would to God they would either conform, or be more wise, and not be catch'd!"

But, Samuel Pepys, they had no other choice! They were not creatures of circumstances, but of conviction. They were upholding the crown rights of their redeemer—they could not muffle the voice of their consciences even at the approach of the police—and, but for them, there would be no democracy in England and no toleration. "Be ye not conformed to this world." That was their new inspiration and strength.

The religion of Jesus Christ has never been spread by "yes-men." The first disciples boldly cried: "We must obey God and not men." Perpetua, the North African martyr, would not listen to her parents' request that she should offer sacrifice to the Roman Emperor as to God. She brushed aside their pleading with the words: "I must be true to my Christian name—Perpetua—constant." Martin Luther was threatened that if he proclaimed his Protestantism in the Council at Worms, he would not come back alive. He retorted: "If I had heard that as many devils would set on me at Worms as there are tiles on the roof, still I would go there." That is the authentic Christian cry. "Be not conformed to this world!"

We shall not be called upon to make the supreme sacrifice of martyrdom, I imagine. But there are many ways in which we are conformed to this world, which must be transformed to the good and acceptable and perfect will of God. Let me give a few examples.

IN THE WORLD OF THE MIND

A great change is desirable here. We no longer take God's Word as our authority in the world of the mind. A hundred years ago, Christians used to say: "What does God think of me?" Today, we say: "What do I think of God?" It is an impudent and impertinent change. You see this attitude in the way not only laymen, but bishops, wait anxiously for the pronouncements of the scientists, before deciding how much of the Christian creed is still tenable. Are we to base our lives on the latest pronouncements of Julian Huxley or Waddington or on the eternal truth revealed by the eternal Son of God?

I think this is an important question. To hang on the lips of the scientists, as if God needs their confirmation, is a form of unbelief. It is also folly. For "Science sheds its last year's conclusions as a snake its skin, or a crab its shell."

I see the same spirit in those who flaunt the negatives in their belief: "I cannot accept the miracles." Or "I find it impossible to accept the Genesis account of the creation." Or "The Resurrection makes too much demand on my credulity." Or "I like to keep an open mind in such matters." My friends, as G. K. Chesterton once said, there is only one point in having an open mind, as in having an open mouth, namely to shut it on something solid. And the Christian is the man or woman who is committed to believing in the miracles of the Incarnation: that God was incarnate and came to earth.

In the kingdom of the mind—to the great detriment of our faith—we combine an adult knowledge of science with a juvenile knowledge of the Word of God. His Word is a lamp unto our feet and we prefer the flashy torches of modern men.

"The word was made flesh and dwelt among us"—that is the intellectual charter of our faith. Our authority is God's. In God's name, let us cease toadying and spanielling to the scientists. "Be ye not conformed to this world, but be ye transformed by the renewing of your mind, that ye may prove what is the good, and acceptable, and perfect will of God."

IN THE LIFE OF THE CHURCH

I see one way in the Church in which we have conformed to the ways of the world: snobbery.

The Church should be the one place in the world where the world's distinctions are left in the porch when we enter; where every man and woman can be sure of a real welcome, not simply formal politeness. But there is constant complaint that new-comers are elbowed out or cold-shouldered. As a warning, let me recount a story from Angus Watson's *My Life*.

A colored man who had been most successful in his business career applied for admission to the Fifth Avenue Presbyterian Church, New York. The minister said to him: "My Church is made up entirely of white members and it is the most prosperous Church in New York. If I were to admit you to membership, I should split the church from top to bottom. I think you'd better go and talk to God about the whole matter and come and see me in a fortnight."

Several months passed and the minister met the colored man in the street. "Mr. Johnson," said the minister, "you didn't come again to see me about that business we spoke of." "No," replied the Negro. "I haven't come back and I ain't coming back. I did just what you said. I went and talked to God about the whole business and he said: 'What's that, Mr. Johnson, you want to become a member of Fifth Avenue Presbyterian Church? Why, sir? I've been trying to get into that Church myself for the last five years.'"

This is a parable. Any church that refuses admission or welcome to a man because he is poor or because he belongs to another race is barring its doors against God and his Church. "There is neither Jew, nor Greek," says God's word; and God help us if we raise human barriers, when God has done away with them. "God is no respecter of persons," says God's Word, and the Church that is a respecter of persons is no Church of God, but a dominion of Satan! "Be ye not conformed to this world." That means regarding every man, woman, or child who enters this church as one for whom Christ died, and who has a right to expect love, understanding, and friendship as the world cannot give. Neglect this, at your peril!

IN FACING DIFFICULTIES AND DEATH

I fear that we wreck the Christian Church in our daily life often by our attitude to difficulty and death. Faced with these situations, we complain like the outsider: "Why doesn't God intervene?" or "God has failed me." Are these the accents of faith? Does this sound like the followers of him who said: "In this world ye shall have tribulation, but be of good cheer, I have overcome the world." And, in our burial services where the muted drums of sadness drown the Christian trumpets of Resurrection, we are again conforming to this world. We believe in the Resurrection and the Life to come—then let us show the world by our faith and courage that we do. The way to face death or bereavement as a Christian was finally shown by a Canadian soldier. He saw his best friend blown to pieces by a shell. Standing silent for a moment he said: "It will take more than that to stop you."

My friends I bid you: "Be not conformed to this world, but be ye transformed to the good, and acceptable, and perfect will of God." That means a life lifted out of the rut of selfishness; that means a life lived after the example of the glorious Prince of Life, the Christ; that means eternal life here and hereafter. That also means entering into the crucifixion of Christ, in suffering, and into the Resurrection of Christ, in hope. In the words of St. Paul: "Be ye conformed to the image of God's Son."

Then in God's name, nail your colors to the mast! Live for Christ and speak up for Christ!

11

Retrospect

A New Year Sermon, Preached in Wallington, London

Ministers, answerable to God about the spiritual feeding of his sheep, are concerned with attendance at church. However, considering requests for changes in the preaching—a simpler Gospel, a simpler mode of delivery, a more pietistic or evangelical homily—does not preclude the minister's leadership in tradition and modernity and the fact that a practical, ethical and sensible religion, telling the hard truth, might arouse parishioners from lethargy. Indeed twentieth-century man may not have a "conversion story," but may need to lay down the modern burdens of perplexity, boredom and sadness at the foot of the Cross and meet Christ face to face. Overwhelmed by a sense of inadequacy in the face of the problems of the world, he looks for a vision, trust in the Lord, and peace.

> Psalm 90:4: "For a thousand years in thy sight are but as a yesterday when it is past, and as a watch in the night."

THE SADDEST OF ALL sounds is the midnight bell tolling out the old year. We are all older by twelve months, but not wiser. We are all one milestone further on life's pilgrimage, but not all have the strength to complete it. It is a time for brooding reflection. The shopkeepers are stock-taking. And we should be spiritually taking stock of our resources.

It is good to remember as we say goodbye to the old year, whatever our witness has been, that in cities and towns and villages, on the high seas, in concentration-camps, faithful witness has been borne to Christ and his Gospel.

What are your thoughts in the pew? Do you sometimes think what your minister's thoughts must be? Do you ever think that he shudders when he rises on a cold and wet morning, knowing that because of the weather, many that Sunday are going to leave God out in the cold and stay at home fire-watching? Do you ever think, when he is absent from the pulpit, that in the other church where he is preaching, he hopes against hope that you will show your steadfastness to Christ by attending? Do you ever know, I wonder, the intense gladness with which he reacts when one of you comes in all seriousness and says "I feel that it would be wrong of me to stay out of Church-membership. Christ needs us all to pull together"? Do you ever feel the shock of shame or happy surprise I feel when I turn the corner behind the choir and see either pews or faces predominate? I am telling you these things because we are partners in God's enterprise here. If the congregations fail, then I am failing, and you are failing. If the congregations are good, then we together are succeeding in our witness.

Perhaps some of you think I am asking for too much. I know you try to help with your reasons for the sparseness of the congregations: influenza, the preponderance of the aged, or whatever it is. Now see my side of the picture. I am not content to plod along; certainly not to mark time. This is not the normal pace of the Army of Christ. If it is not marching, it is retreating. That is why I urge you on. I dare not face God and say: "This is the best that I could do. I tried to put a good face on things. Other churches have done worse, Lord." Swift would come the divine answer: "What is that to thee? Feed my sheep."

Now when we have spoken a word of thanksgiving for the solid achievements of a year's ministry in which we all shared, we shall do well to thrust the past aside with a fierce impatience. We must do more.

1. To begin with, what more can I do as a preacher? In this New Year shall I try something different, or do something more in my preaching? I am convinced that a minister's sermons are reflected in his people. It is a cooperative effort.

Now suppose that we realize that Christ has commissioned us to a new campaign for his kingdom? Suppose that we are fiercely impatient with the slow plodding of the past and we are resolved to make a bid for a more resounding victory, where should we begin?

I hear someone say: "Start in the pulpit. Begin to speak the language of the people." It may be that I have to change the tone of the sermon and do as some of our leaders tell me: "Give evangelistic addresses of a purely spiritual tone." "Win men to Christ, who shall win others." Now that is absolutely central in any worthy ministry. We must strike for a decision with the evangelical appeal. As Protestants, we must be evangelical or nothing. Our religion may be liberal or orthodox in its formal definitions, but it has no meaning unless it brings men face to face with God as revealed in Jesus Christ. The central truth is the good news that in communion with God we can find liberation from sin and fear.

It seems easy to grant the truth of the contention: "Preach evangelistic addresses. Win men and women for Christ." But there is a hidden danger in this oversimplification. One of the dangers as I see it is this. We assume in the listener a sense of his own sinfulness and need, which he does not really possess.

Let us be honest with ourselves about this. I believe the sense of sin, of spiritual inadequacy is still a part of every deep and complete spiritual experience; but the reality of sin in the individual experience does not loom as large as it did in the days of Bunyan, Wesley or Spurgeon. They all felt that they were sinners because they were rebels of Adam's breed. They might reject religion or accept it, but they knew that the first step towards religion was the renouncing of their sin.

Now this is not the mood in which modern men listen to the preacher of today. Men and women have accepted life. We are not afraid of any of our faculties. We do not think our instincts are naturally evil. We are not afraid of beauty and pleasure and comfort as snares. We claim that they are good; in fact, we claim them as part of our birthright.

The difference today is just this: people turn to religion not because of bad past or bad parts, but because of good parts. They know that life is a good thing, but that life at its best is not good enough without God. We feel possibilities and aspirations within ourselves that are meaningless without God. We are in revolt against the injustices and agonies of life, and with this challenge on our lips we turn to God beyond this dark veil. We want to better the world, but we realize that our goodness is too weak unless it is reinforced by heavenly power.

Now this is not a universal mood; but it is sufficiently general today to call for something different from the old simple call for repentance.

Now the unchanging element in evangelical preaching is the invitation to men and women to lay their burdens at the feet of Christ. It may not be today the burden of conscious sin. It may be the burden of intellectual perplexity; or the burden of a heart pierced by the sorrows of humanity; or the burden of a mind unsatisfied with the pleasures of life and activities of life unrelated to any eternal purpose.

The message we have to give these folks as minister and people is this: peace for heart and mind and will in the all-embracing purpose of God's love and the promise of power through the living spirit of God.

How can I make that message vital and dynamic? Will topical preaching do it? Will sermon-lectures on psychology or economics do it? I like to deal with these facts of modern life and thought. But to think only on these lines is to assume that the Gospel is out-of-date. But the function of the preacher is to preach Christ, and [Christ] crucified.

People will not come to the churches for any other purpose for long. All around men and women through the week are hearing the clang and clamor of material realities. The spiritual world seems far away, and the voice of the spirit within is faint as bells pealing across the untroubled waters of a lake.

For whatever reason a man clings to his faith in God—for consolation, for guidance, or for power to resist evil—it is not in the world of business that he will find encouragement to hold fast to such a faith.

A man looking around the world today would find it hard to see any evidence of the thought of God reflected in the ways of men. Newman said, as one who had searched the faces of men for some reflection of God in them: "It is as if I looked into a mirror and did not see my face."

Friends of the Churches and disciples of Christ, this is our glorious service—to feed the starved souls of men with bread that the world cannot give. Our gift is faith: the faith that comforts; the faith that provides an anchor for the soul amid the winds and waves of life; the faith that casts out fear and sin; the faith that makes life worth living; the faith that alone makes life possible.

2. Now let us look at another suggestion for more effective preaching. Some people say: "Preach the simple gospel." I do not know exactly what that means, but I think I know what they want, who ask for the simple Gospel. It is a kind of dainty music played into the ears of complacent saints as comfort for the individual soul within the Church. My friends, that is the easiest type of preaching imaginable. How fatally facile it is to preach poetry and compose fine phrases and silken terms. But this is to use language as a means of hiding, not exposing thought.

I believe that I am commissioned to preach a practical, ethical, sensible religion, which is not less the good news for that. It is good news because it rouses man from his lethargy with stern demands. I will not, even if you demand it, sing you a soothing lullaby.

What the world hungers for, when it turns to religion, is some strong assurance that the things of the spirit are truly and marvelously real. Marvelously? Yes, unbelievably so! Men come to believe in Christ, to believe with him and at last to stake their lives on that belief.

3. One last thought as we face the future.

In preaching and practice, I would ask for a more complete reliance upon the power of Christ: "I, if I be lifted up, will draw all men unto me," so said our blessed Lord in utter confidence as he faced the grievous path to the Cross.

Our joint job must be to lift up Christ, placard him, and pester him in our lives—to draw all men to him, and to continue in his power. We are called to this primary task, and to a more resolute avoidance of the side-issues of religion.

If I have disappointed some of you, because my preaching was unequal, because it was not always studded with illustrations or startling thoughts; if I have disappointed others because I did not preach nice, innocent sermons, pretty and evasive and vague, but I chose instead to sear your conscience: or to demand that Christianity enter into politics to claim this sphere for Christ, I cannot apologize. I have chosen to preach as I do because I am neither a contributor to *Punch*, nor a Wilhelmina Stitch, nor a purveyor of patent medicine, nor an anesthetist. It is my more difficult task to preach the Christian Gospel which tells the whole truth, the often painful truth, but the truth that shall make you free.

You come to church not to be taught to behave properly. You come to church to learn why you should bother about behavior at all; why you should follow an unseen Lord and why you should subdue your thoughts and deeds to the laws of the invisible Kingdom.

You do not come to church to learn how to be respectably sensible. You come to Church to find a reason for being nobly mad, so mad as to be ready to surrender your very lives for the sake of a vision and a dream. A vision of Christ like men, a vision of a world of brothers living in community, a vision of God's Kingdom established here in England. I know that in the routine stuffiness of an office, or in the mutual compact of silence in the train, this Kingdom seems remote, impossible. But this Kingdom will come, not in England's green and pleasant land, but in the slums of

Southwark and the Rhondda Valley, amidst the factories of Birmingham and Bradford. And you and I are going to keep that vision vivid as our splendid gift to an apathetic world.

My beloved people, if we have that gift in our eyes, let us proclaim it simply, urgently, incessantly. Think what it might mean here if such a congregation went out to preach and to live for such a vision. What would happen? I would not venture to place any limits on the possibilities of God's power unleashed in us.

We dedicate our lives afresh to this high calling as we look down upon the faces of the men and women as yet unknown to us, for whom in the year that is dawning we shall break the bread of life and pour the wine of eternity.

12

Christianity in the Atomic Age

Preached in Wallington, London at the time of the Bombing of Japan, and in 1946

This sermon expresses the indignation of the preacher on hearing the news of the bombing of Japan in August 1945, the cries of despair emanating from famous European thinkers, and the despondency of the British Council of Churches, whose report was published officially in 1946. The second part of the sermon attempts to restore hope that humanity will be brought to its knees in humility and repentance after this wake-up call, ban the destructive use of enriched uranium and place the new discoveries of science and energy at the service of all men.

- Zechariah 4:6: "This is the word of the LORD unto Zerubbabel, saying: 'Not by might, nor by power, but by my spirit,' saith the LORD of hosts."

- Daniel 2:20: "Blessed be the name of God for ever and ever; for wisdom and might are his . . ."

    2:22: "He revealeth the deep and sacred things: he knoweth what is in the darkness, and the light dwelleth with him."

IN 1919 SIR OLIVER Lodge made a prophecy. Speaking to a group of British scientists of the latent energy in matter, he said: "There is enough power in a handful of common earth to blow the cities of the world to dust. But thank God, we don't know the secret."

Now we do know the secret and the results. For the first time terrible experiments have been carried out and two large industrial cities in Japan have been actually annihilated, by the largest mass-murders the world has ever known. And weeks after the explosions, men and women and children wasted to death from the after effects of the atomic bombs.

To my mind, that was the worst news we heard during the whole of the tragic war years. Many things touched our consciences during those years: chief amongst them the gassing of millions of Jews, men, women and little children in concentration camps like Auschwitz, and the intolerable cruelties of Belsen; the inhumane treatment of our prisoners-of-war, unable to defend themselves. These things cut deep. But the most diabolical act of them all was the indiscriminate use of the atomic bomb on Nagasaki and Hiroshima. That hurt most of all. And do you know why? Because of the damnable hypocrisy of the Allies of the United States and the British Commonwealth of Nations. We, mind you, who had condemned the indiscriminate bombing of Coventry and London and Plymouth and Hull and Southampton, we committed the most flagrant act of indiscriminate warfare, in sending hundreds of thousands of men, women and children to their doom in two nights. We, who called the war a crusade and fought it for liberty, and sent our sons to sacrifice and die for liberty and justice, we did this thing that is the blackest deed in all history.

No wonder the conscience of the Christian world has been scandalized by it. No wonder that the Roman Catholic Father Ronald Knox declares in his essay, "God and the Atom," that the use of the bomb on Hiroshima without a preliminary harmless warning demonstration of its power has lowered our self-respect. No wonder either, that many churchmen in the United States are already planning a campaign for funds to rebuild these cities as costly acts of self-imposed reparation. This thing has seared the conscience of the world. Statesmen may argue that this did in effect shorten the war, and that it saved thousands of allied lives that would have been lost in the invasion of Japan. That is true. But is does not destroy the fact that the liberators of the world proved to be massmurderers. We had a military conquest, but a moral defeat.

But what of the atomic bomb and the future? I am not exaggerating when I say that many distinguished men can see no future at all. H. G. Wells sees no light in the darkness. It is midnight without a morning star for him. He is terrified lest his gruesome pictures of the future will become true and man will commit racial suicide, blowing the brains of the race out in a world atomic war. And the frightened scientists themselves are the first to admit that they can see no defense against this latest weapon of destruction.

Now what are we going to say to these things as Christians. Is this going to shake our Christian faith?

God is the creator of the world. The scientists are only discovering an energy that he has put into it... The book of Genesis tells us that when he made the world, he saw that it was good. Atomic energy, viewed from the Christian standpoint, is a further proof of the immense power of God that has been lying in the atom during thousands of years, waiting for man to discover it, waiting for man to harness it for the benefit of mankind.

We can say with Daniel, meditating on the deep wisdom of God, "Blessed be the name of God forever; for wisdom and might are his... He revealeth the deep and secret things: he knoweth what is in the darkness, and the light dwelleth in Him." God made this power and it is good. It has been used for destruction; but it can be used to provide benefits for mankind, to provide the motive force of a constructive civilization. This is no surprise to God.

The second thing we can say is this! The atomic bomb is the warning finger of God. Spoiled children are disobedient children; their parents may cajole them or threaten them, but all to no purpose. But a frightened child runs to its father for protection. I believe that the fear that has come into the world of the atomic bomb is the threat that may drive the world to God. For never have we seen our helplessness as in this atomic age. Never have we seen more clearly that the really terrifying thing is not bombs, or gas, or a bacillus spray, but just the human hand that releases these things. It is the callousness and cruelty of man that is to be feared and we have lost faith in man.

That is the first step towards faith in God. As the saintly George Herbert put it:

> That, at last,
> If goodness lead him not, yet weariness
> May toss him to my breast.

The explosions of the atomic bomb may, in the providence of God, have an unexpected result; they may detonate and shatter the hard crust of human self-satisfaction and pride, and throw humanity on its knees.

There was a striking notice outside a London Church in the days of the blitz. "If your knees are knocking, kneel on them." The threat of the atomic bomb is God's way of making our knees knock, that we may kneel on them. It has made the Christian faith even more necessary.

It means that the Christians have a stronger incentive than ever for winning men for Christ. For it is only by eradicating the rebel in the souls of men, that the world will be safe. Man is fallen man, bent on his own selfishness, until he is called to halt and to repent by Christ. Nothing less is needed than redemption, a complete change of heart and mind, in fact a revolution in the inner man. That is something that the legislators and the scientists cannot effect. That is the work of God alone and his Church.

There is a text here that should be in our minds these days because it gets to the root of the problem: "The word of God came to Zerubbabel saying not by might, nor by power, but by my Spirit, saith the Lord of Hosts." I want to put side by side with that the confession of a man who has tried to use power and might to coerce men to his views and failed. In his exile in Corsica, Napoleon said:

> Do you know what amazes me more than anything else? The impotence of force to organize anything. There are only two powers in the world: the spirit and the sword. In the long run the sword will always be conquered by the spirit.

Today is the Church's greatest day of opportunity; for men know the importance of the sword and their own impotence.

What shall be our attitude? Find the answer in the *Era of Atomic Power*, the report prepared by the British Council of Churches.

This says: "The Christian attitude to the world is one which takes life in this world seriously and yet not too seriously; an attitude of caring intensely and yet not caring too much..."

The city of God remaineth; the things that are eternal will not be shaken and man, as the child of God, belongs to the eternal world.

13

No Apologies

A Post War Sermon, Preached in Wallington, London

The Christian soldier, we are told, should wield the sword of the Spirit. Beyond the superficial appearance of social differences lie the same basic human needs. Facing the selfishness of nations and power, the Christian must reaffirm allegiance to God and love of neighbor in promoting education, housing and world-peace, and in eradicating prostitution and drugs, as well as racial prejudice and class warfare. By remembering his mortality and trusting in God, the Christian will overcome the discouragement that comes from the realization that sin is ingrained in the self, not just in the hatred and greed of the world, and fighting for righteousness will awaken the hero within him or herself.

- Romans 1:16: "For I am not ashamed of the Gospel of Christ: for it is the power of God unto salvation."

OUR FAITH IS A fighting faith. We are armed with the most powerful secret weapon known: the sword of the Spirit, which is the Word of God. Yet on all sides there is whimpering among the Christian ranks, a defeatism in approach to the gigantic post-war problems, an apology if the Christian faith should offend the susceptibilities of the scientist or the plans of the politicians. By contrast here is St. Paul, trumpeting from the house-tops: "I am not ashamed of the Gospel of Christ, for it is the power of God unto salvation."

By all means, face up realistically to the overwhelming tasks before us. These are our objectives: to secure world-peace, to make universal a higher standard of education, to provide decent houses and to abolish blind-alley occupation, to outlaw race and class warfare: these are gigantic tasks and, in comparison, the numbers of effective Christians seem feeble to cope with them.

See how St. Paul tackled an equally difficult situation and wanted eagerly to go to Rome, the proud city of the imperial Caesar. What an intrepid spirit it required to go to Rome and to say to its citizens: "I have something more worthy of your allegiance than empires and armies, and wealth, and grandeur, and learning." Yet that was St. Paul's claim. "Hence" he wrote, "my eagerness to preach the Gospel to you in Rome also, for I am proud of the Gospel of Christ."

We need this militant, challenging note in Christianity today, the Spirit that dares to throw down the gauntlet to the world's power and greatness.

I want with you to celebrate those elements of the Christian Gospel which merit our boasting in them.

1. The Christian need not be ashamed that in his Gospel all men are equal in the sight of God. God is unimpressed by a man's talent, position, fame, wealth, or achievement. The Christian Gospel goes down below the surfaces of men and women and their differences, and sees that all are alike at heart in their deepest needs and desires, their aspirations and hopes, their temptations and failures. All men are leveled in the sight of Christ; and that is what caused so much of the resentment and bitterness against our Lord during his earthly life. For him, a poor woman drawing water at the well was as important as the Pharisee. He was utterly unimpressed by wealth. When he saw a poor widow casting in two farthings into the Temple Treasury alongside the lavish gifts of the wealthy, he said: "This woman hath cast in more than them all, for in her poverty she hath cast in all that she hath." We need not be ashamed of Christ's viewpoint of human nature: there is only one standard by which to judge people that is not superficial—to judge them as children of God.

"Fading is the worldling's pleasure." Christ's followers have always known that. When Louis XIV died, after his luxurious and splendid reign, courtiers and dignitaries assembled to pay him their last respects. The cathedral church of Notre-Dame was decorated to form a great pall for his coffin. The preacher ascended the pulpit, and all movement ceased as they fixed their eyes upon him. Wars, arts, and pageantry passed before their eyes, all the amazing triumphs and changes of these seventy-five years, as they wondered how the preacher would deal with them. And then, after a pause, his first words shattered them: "Only God is great!" Men had come to have their pride stimulated, to listen to great words of man; they had been brought face to face with God, who is no respecter of persons.

The poorest and humblest person may enter the secret place of prayer and meet the Father who sees in secret. And the highest and most exalted person in history can enter only by the same way of humility and penitence and recognition of unworthiness.

In an age when men are murdered in their millions, when they are dragooned by dictators and reduced to statistics by economists, I am not ashamed of the Gospel of Jesus Christ in which all men are equal—equal in need of forgiveness and grace; equal in their sanctity and worth because Christ died for all.

2. I am not ashamed of the Gospel of Christ because it claims an authority higher than the world's highest. It claims obedience to God rather than to men. No one knew that better than St. Paul. For conscience's sake he stood against the world's mightiest men, and went to his death unconquered. To obey God has always meant opposition from the world, from the time that Christ carried his Cross and challenged the evil of men from it. In all ages men and women have gladly accepted the same Cross for the sake of remaining true to their Master. We need never be ashamed of such an uncompromising loyalty of conscience.

In a world organized on a selfish basis, the Christian's duty is to sound that sustained note of unflinching loyalty. There are many things in personal, social and national life that we cannot condone. Indeed we must get beyond that negative attitude and say: so long as there is sin in the world, it is not a reason for despair, but a challenge to conquer until the whole of life is guided by the spirit and values of Christ.

The Apostle is proud of the Gospel because it equalizes all men in the sight of God, because it puts obedience to God before obedience to men, and also because it gives man power over forces of evil that are normally too strong for him.

3. "It is the power of God unto salvation." No experience in life is more devastating than when a man realizes that he is up against forces that are too strong for him in his own make-up. The truth, as the Psalmist knew it, breeds sheer despair: "My sins are stronger than I." This too, Paul knew for himself. In this very letter to the Romans he paints a vivid picture of

his futile fight with himself to attain his ideals. "O wretched man that I am. Who shall deliver me from the body of this death?" But the fight did not end there. When Christ laid hold of him, the tide of battle turned, and when he fought now in the might of the strong Son of God, the cry changed: "Thanks be unto God who hath given us the victory through our Lord Jesus Christ." Little wonder that Paul's message flamed across a sin-weary world like a prairie fire.

The greatest need today is such power to overcome. Human sin has always been loathsome but never more than today when science has put at its disposal powers fit only for gods. Hatred has always been destructive, but today it kindles the whole world ablaze, and exterminates two and a half million Jews. Greed has always been ruthless but today it can deprive millions of work and food and houses to fill the pockets of the few. Yes, evil forces have been too strong for men, but now more than ever.

If we who are Christ's know the victory God gives, how dare we be silent or apologetic? St. Paul would find it hard to understand such apathy and lifeless witness as we so often show. Such a Gospel and such a challenge, he knew, demanded a great deal from its followers. But he believed that people had it in them to respond. In those days the cost of discipleship was greater than it is today. It usually meant criticism; not infrequently it meant torture, crucifixion, or being thrown to the lions. But that did not daunt them. A young boy was passing into the arena to be mauled to death by lions, just for the perverted amusement of Roman society. As he passed the door a Roman soldier sneered: "And where is your carpenter's Son now?" Quick as lightening came back the reply: "Making a coffin for your emperor."

I do not believe that the heroic spirit is dead in people. The Battle of Britain, the epic of Arnhem, the defeat of the Graf Spee, the convoys to Malta and Murmansk are proof that bravery is alive among us. Would that we Christians at home had half the pluck and the daring of those who defend us! I believe that we might develop it. I am convinced that the hero Christ can still capture men by the sheer daring of his demands upon them. For he claims all or nothing. His command is total obedience. And the hero in the heart of everyman longs to answer: "Lord, what wilt thou have me to do?"

According to W. L. Hunton:

> Fading is the worldling's pleasure,
> All his boasted pomp and show;
> Solid joys and lasting treasure
> None but Zion's children know.
>
> —John Newton

14

Eternal Life: Heaven and Hell

An Evening Homily, Preached in Wallington, London

Though stating that "fire and brimstone" sermons are no longer fashionable, this homily reasserts the importance of judgment within the Christian faith, affirmed by the heart and by the need for repentance before being granted Christ's forgiveness. It presents heaven and hell in the here and now, probes the darker side of our souls, so ready to persecute, and stresses salvation by faith, in the acceptance of Christ and of his Way. Sheep and goats, light and darkness, heaven and hell are seen here both as realities and metaphor—judgments on individuals, nations, and history.

- Matthew 25:31–4: "When the Son of man shall come in his glory, and all the holy angels with him, then shall he sit upon the throne of his glory: And before him shall be gathered all nations: and he shall separate them one from another, as a shepherd divideth his sheep from the goats: And he shall set the sheep on his right hand, but the goats on the left. Then the king will say to those on his right: 'Come, my Father has blessed you! Inherit the kingdom prepared for you from the creation of the world.'"

- John 3:19–21: "And this is the condemnation, that light is come into the world, and men loved darkness rather than light, because their deeds were evil. For every one that doeth evil hateth the light, neither cometh to the light, lest his deeds should be reproved. But he that doeth truth cometh to the light, that his deeds may be made manifest, that they are wrought in God."

WHEN THAT CHOICE SPIRIT, Quiller-Couch, whose novels and essays have delighted the discerning for the past thirty years, penned his boyhood memories, one terrible nightmare cast its shadow over him. When he was twelve or thirteen, he went to the Congregational Church at Newton Abbot. The eloquent preacher and minister of that church, painted, he says: "Hell for us, its fires and tortures everlasting, as vividly as though he, an eye-witness, had of late been there and barely escaped back across the one narrow bridge over the pit." Quiller-Couch adds: "I dare say the man was honest. What I know is that for two or three years this preacher so affected a child that he would wake and grip the bed clothes to hold back a scream." It was not for himself he was afraid but for his father and mother, with their easy-going religious ways that he "awoke sweating from dreams of them in torture."

That kind of preaching has gone. It has gone because it is not the purpose of our Faith to offer men salvation as a fire-escape. It has gone because its conception of God and of our Lord was vindictive, cruel and unworthy. But, and here lies the mistake, we have rejected the Christian doctrine of judgment because the imagery in which it was clothed was liable to be crudely used. We have—I am speaking of Christians generally—refused the teaching because the book was badly illustrated. And in the place of that essential teaching on Judgment, we have substituted the immoral and sentimental idea that everything is bound to come out right at the end.

I want to remind you tonight that it is not the details of the pictures that matter; it is inevitable that we use pictures because we are pictures of time and we cannot think of eternity except in pictures. But I am reminded by one of the greatest Biblical teachers of today in his Gifford Lectures: "It is unwise for Christians to claim any knowledge of either the furniture of heaven or the temperature of hell; or to be too certain of any details of the Kingdom of God in which history is consummated. But it is prudent to accept the testimony of the heart, which affirms the fear of judgment." (Niebuhr, *The Nature and Destiny of Man* (1941–1943). II. 304.)

The New Testament presents us with two judgments: the one present and the one after this life. It reminds us that for each of us death is inevitable, but that arriving at the destination God offers to us is not inevitable.

1. We are solemnly reminded that we are men being judged now by our response to God's eternal Son. "For God sent not his Son into the world to be judged by the world, but that the world should be saved through him." The result is that "He that believeth in him is not judged." He is pardoned because he has repented and accepted the amazing love of Christ. But the other result is this: "He that believeth not has been judged already, because he hath not believed in the name of the only begotten Son of God."

The shifting of the ways, the division, goes on now. Hell and heaven are not simply future destinations; they are that; but here and now the choice is made. To be or not to be with Christ that is the question upon which our destiny hinges. And this is the judgment: "that the light is come into the world and men loved the darkness rather than the light, for their works were evil." I reminded you last Sunday evening that eternal life is fellowship with God and with Christ and it begins here and now, although it finds its full fruition and consummation hereafter. I remind you, by the very words of the Lord of Life that hell begins now, that it is a positive rejection of Christ, and an equally positive preference for evil. There can be no neutrality in this warfare. Indecision and apathy are the certain signs that we have not submitted to the Lordship of Christ.

"He that is not with me is against me." That is the reproof of God's heavenly Son in the flesh. It cannot be argued against. It can be believed or disbelieved.

Even the most apathetic of men and women can see today that destiny is actually determined by belief or disbelief in Jesus Christ. How else can you explain the war in which we are engaged at such cost of life and sacrifice on the battlefields and at home? I know that Hitler could use the name of God in his speeches; but the devil can transform himself into an angel of light and quote Scripture. But his god was the god of his own creation, the god of the German will to power. I believe profoundly that for the sake of the preservation of Britain, or imperialism, or England, home and beauty, and all the rest of it, we should not have been justified in fighting. But for the sake of the Christian values in our civilization, only, had we the right to take up arms. The way is again open for a new advance in the name of Jesus Christ. But for the men whose bodies held back the tides of black paganism, the Church and Christians in the world would have been driven back into the caves.

Conflict between Nazism and the European Christian tradition was as inevitable as conflict between the children of darkness and the children of light. Our men who have been at the front have seen evil triumphant, flaunting its hellish powers. Our fellow Christians in Germany, many of them now with Christ, have known that evil is not a preacher's fancy. It is a power that makes the mind muddy mire, kindliness a trivial sentimentality, a power that hits with truncheons all who are children of the light.

The only possible commentary on *Mein Kampf* and the success of the Nazi regime is: "Men loved the darkness rather than the light." This is history.

Belsen, Buchenwald, Sachsenhausen, Luthin ... You say: "Thank God it can't happen here." But let me remind you, as I remind myself, that the word "man" includes us. I shudder to think of the way that we in this country take our responsibilities lightly to Christ. Men and women, your destiny will not be decided by whether you supported the war effort, by your prime-minister, by your reputation amongst your business associates, not even by your contributions to charities, worthy as these lesser devotions are. It will be, nay, it *is* being decided by your response to Jesus Christ. He is the man of destiny to whom God has committed the keys of death and Hades. Life with him is God's destiny for you, but if you refuse that offer, it will be hell for you in this life. And you will have the agony of separation from God in the life after death, the agony of having failed to meet the love of God with faith and trust.

In *Brighton Rock* Graham Greene writes:

> *Boy*: I don't take any stock in religion. Hell; it's just there. You don't need to think of it, not before you die.
>
> *Girl*: You might die sudden.
>
> *Boy*: You know what they say: "Between the stirrup and the ground, he something sought and something found."
>
> *Girl*: Mercy.
>
> *Boy*: That's right: Mercy.
>
> *Girl*: It would be awful though, if they didn't give you time.

These are grim words. But is there any more grim possibility than to be condemned by the justice of Christ because you loved yourself, your possessions, your business, and your pleasures more than you loved our Lord, and his Church and his people? I am neither ashamed nor afraid to remind you, as I remind myself of these things. For in the last analysis, nothing matters except whether you fulfilled God's purpose in Jesus Christ.

2. I would remind you also of the future Judgment, when the glorified Christ sits augustly on the throne of his glory, to judge the nations. That great Shepherd of the sheep who knows who are his own, and knows who are not his, will confirm his judgment in this light. Who shall be on his

right hand? You are expecting me to say: all the decent people, all the religious people, all the kindly people. No, that is not the promise. It is only for those who entered into the Kingdom of God through the gate of repentance in Jesus Christ and joined his company, then shall the King say to them on his right hand, notice the words carefully: "Come ye, blessed of my Father, inherit the Kingdom prepared for you from the foundation of the world," prepared by Christ when he was in the bosom of the father before the world was made: the Kingdom that came in the history of the Incarnation, death and resurrection, the Kingdom that his brethren, the apostles, went forth to proclaim from house to house and city to city. The decisive issue for the day when Jesus spoke these solemn words was whether his witnesses were received gladly, whether they were fed when hungry, or thirsty, or needed clothes, or were sick or imprisoned.

Loyalty to Christ's witnesses will be accepted as loyalty to him. These are the brethren: "Verily I say unto you. In as much as ye did it unto the least of these, my brethren, ye did it unto me."

The final issue is not whether we have been kind to our fellow men—that is one of the by-products of faith—but whether we have received the witnesses of the Kingdom of God brought in by Jesus Christ, and whether we have proved, by pure loyalty, in loving concern for them, that we accept the good news that they bring. I can put it more briefly. Have we proved our loyalty to our Lord by our loyalty to his Church, which is his body that witnesses to the Gospel?

If we have not, then shall he answer us: "Verily, I say unto you, in as much as ye did it not unto one of the least of these, you did not do it unto me. And these shall go into eternal punishment; but the righteous, who trust not in their own righteousness, but in their adherence to the Lord Christ, shall enter into eternal life."

No one can escape this judgment, because no man escapes death. It is inevitable. But no man can leave this service tonight without knowing that he has not been solemnly warned by his Lord, out of sheer love for him. No woman can leave this service without knowing that, as a witness to the Lord of Life, as a Christian woman, she is urged and compelled to work and pray for the grace of God to bring in souls to that Kingdom prepared from the foundation of the world.

Heaven and hell are, whatever the language we use to describe them, the two and the only two possibilities offered by our Lord. We dare not, in obedience to him, blunt the edge of our witness. We are now at the parting of the ways. May God, through the grace of Jesus Christ, enable us to pass over from the kingdom of darkness into the kingdom of light now, that we and ours may hear the destined promise. Come ye blessed of my father, inherit the kingdom prepared for you from the foundation of the world.

Let us pray:

O my God, who dost bid us halt by the solemn warnings of thy Son, and the costliness of thy love in the Cross, grant us, by the means of grace and the hope of glory, to be born again into thy Kingdom, that we and ours may share the glory of thy heavenly Kingdom, where Christ shall be all in all. Set our feet in the way everlasting. Through Jesus Christ, the Lover and the Judge of all mankind. AMEN.

15

Christ and Individual Need (1)

Notes: Delivered at L.M.S. Swanwick, England

Man needs bread, shelter and work, but he lives neither by bread alone, nor by intelligence and bread alone—knowledge without a conscience can lead to ruin—but needs an answer to the questions raised by sin, suffering and death. Against egotism, Christ came as a servant of God's world; to overcome suffering, Christ chose acceptance; to overcome death, he promised the Resurrection. Christ lives both in time and in eternity.

WHAT ARE THE BASIC needs of man? The satisfaction of the individual's basic drives of sex and hunger, says the biologist who sees the individual as a slightly more complicated animal than a developed ape. Yet there is an element of truth in this, for a loveless human being or a starved human being is only half-human, but so also is a full-bellied and lascivious monarch like Henry VIII. Yes, man has wants like the animals, but, as Dr. Johnson said, "unlike them, he is not satisfied when they are met." Ask the sociologist and he will say that man's basic need is for a better environment—a place in a hygienic community-centre with a good safe job, three good meals a day. Change the environment, take men out of the slums or the kraals or the tenements of Tyneside, Harlem, Tiger Bay, Orlando Township, feed them on a balanced diet, keep them happy by a job with secure prospect and a pension at the end, give them enough over to buy a TV and a Butlin holiday, and you will fulfill their basic needs.

This answer, too, is half-true and half-false. True, because man is not merely an individual, but a being who longs for a decent community existence; false, because he can have all these things and still be discontented. Ask the educator and his answer is that man is an intelligent being and better education will lead to an expanding range of interests and intelligent participation in the world. More schools, better trained teachers, and the basic intellectual need of the individual is satisfied. Again, the answer is partly true, partly false. It is true because man's intelligence is one of the characteristics which distinguishes him from the animals, and until a person is educated, his potentialities are not known. It is false because education is neutral and may lead to the making of smart Alecs, or clever devils. ("Because, teacher, I'm smart and they're dumb.")

All the answers to the question: "What is man's basic need?" are criticized by the Christian theologian because they are partial, not comprehensive. They do not deal with man on the deepest level: they blink at three hard, inescapable facts which that most honest of books, the Bible, does not shrink from: the facts of sin, suffering, and death. Now the Christian claim is that every person can live, by faith or trust in Jesus Christ, a life—whatever the time or period of life and whatever the sex or culture or nationality—which overcomes the tragic realities of sin, suffering, and death. And it is this Christian Realism that I want to expound to you in the first lecture.

The obedience of faith is centered on the Cross and the Resurrection of the Messiah and Lord of History, Jesus Christ. The denial of all utopian, blithe, canary-like chirping optimism is the Cross. Men put the Holy and Eternal Son of God to death, and not unspeakable black guards, but ordinary selfish men and women let him die. That fact alone would lead to despair and cynicism. But the Cross does reveal the destructive character of egotism. Man is a crucifier, a murderer, and a slow murderer. But the Resurrection is the denial of all pessimism, for when men had done their worst, and tried to close His mouth for ever in the dust of the grave; God raised him from the dead, and has thereby declared that: "This is indeed my beloved son." That is what I mean by Christian Realism.

We know the worst and the best about man, and that the worst, by the power of the risen and transforming Christ can be made extraordinary.

Now the real test of the Saviorhood of Jesus Christ is what he can do in us to overcome that rebellion in us that we call sin, that suffering, mental, emotional, physical, which flesh is heir to, and that ultimate anxiety and fear from which even the youngest of us is not liberated, the fear of death. If these enemies of man can be overcome in us by Jesus Christ, then he is indeed, Jesus Christ, the same yesterday, today, yea and forever. He is, indeed, not he, but "Thou," the rightful Lord of my life, and I am his grateful servant.

Who is Jesus Christ?

The incarnate Lord. Now we know what God is like. You have this mind in you which was also in Christ Jesus, who, though he was on equality with God, thought it not a thing to be grasped at, but emptied himself, taking the form of a servant . . .

The Prince got out and walked . . .

Jesus, knowing that He came from God and went to God, took a towel and girded himself . . .

In him we see the eternal Son of God, in the flesh: what God is, what man does to God, what man can be.

Christus Victor

1. Over sin: Old Adam versus New Adam. Saul becomes Paul. Sin is rebellion against God. He shows me what sin does. He accepts the worst that sin can do. He shows the love.

2. Over suffering: Alfonso Rodriguez (p. 118, missions under the Cross).

3. Over death: (Abraham—an Indian—finds Christ). (J. Leslie Newbigin *South India Diary*, 38). For a sculpture see Epstein's Lazarus. See J. S. Bach: *St. John's Passion* . . . "It will do more than that to stop God" (The Canadian soldier). "If we suffer with Him, we shall reign with Him." I and Thou: "Thou must increase, I must decrease."

The mighty acts and facts of God in Christ: he is our eternal contemporary, Savior, and Exemplar.

16

Christ and Individual Need (2): Thou and They
Delivered at L.M.S. Swanwick, England

Based on Jesus's two commandments, this oration first contrasts the dangers of bias, in pietism as well as in socialism and the social gospel, before insisting on the need for convergence of the temporal and the religious, and on the importance of community in the Church. The facets of the theme are kaleidoscopically viewed through history, socialism, the thinkers of the Church, and brought together in an appraisal of the doctrine of the Incarnation.

I FEAR THAT I shall, without your concentration, become a mere lecturer today: one who talks in other people's sleep.

The great ex-Communist and former professor of Philosophy at Moscow University, Berdyaev, has reminded us that the Christian faith means Communion and Community. There is a fundamental vertical relationship between Thou, God and Me, but it is incomplete unless there is a horizontal relationship between Me and Them, which is fully a triangular relationship between God (Thou), Me and Them. I can put it briefly by saying that the Christian faith is love of God in Christ and love of my neighbor through the response of finding him to be my neighbor, because Christ is his elder brother and mine. Our equality is found in the fact that we are Christ's brothers. Our Christian faith is both individual and communal, both this-worldly and other-worldly.

And if the danger of pietism is that it is too much interested in souls (not souls-in-bodies, and not souls-in-bodies in their environmental context), Bonhoeffer speaks of the folly of taking temperature all the time. The danger of the social gospel is that it is so much interested in the community and in the here and now that it neglects the soul and neglects the hereafter.

The Pietist with his smug hymn: "O it will be glory for me" or the ecclesiastical with his war-cry: "It's your souls we want," seals himself and sees the half of the truth, ignoring the cry from the poor of Boston: "Give us half a crown now." Equally, the social gospeller sees only the other half of the truth with his slogan: "The kingdom of God is social justice." But in a Britain which has recently heard a remarkable pietist with a transatlantic accent, a face like Van Heflin and electronic aids in his lapel—you know whom I mean—the truth of the social gospel needs to be reaffirmed, and that is what I want to begin to do in this lecture. Let me call it the social implications of the Gospel.

First, the first preaching of the Gospel created a community of the Holy Spirit. It created a communism of believers. They were not only of one mind; they did not only worship one crucified, risen, and regnant Lord; they were not only empowered with one interior Holy Spirit (the Fellowship of the Holy Spirit); they were not only united in entering the community of the faithful by the one baptismal rite by which they symbolized that they were buried with Christ under the waters of Baptism, and joined with the Risen Christ the leader of the new race, as they emerged from the waters; they even had all things, all goods common. And this spiritual communism, this voluntary communism which arose, not from class-hatred, but from the transformation of class-divisions in Christ, has haunted the Christian Church ever since.

In monasteries, Eastern and Western, there was an attempt to establish a community of property, but corporate wealth in time corrupts the primal intention. And anyway, unlike the spiritual communism of the Acts, it was not a family communism, but one divided sexually into brotherhoods and sisterhoods apart. Then the Franciscan Friars emulated the simplicity of Christ as they wandered from place to place without a permanent home. In fifteenth century Holland, the brotherhoods led a communist life. The poor preachers of England, the Lollards and followers of Wycliffe protested against the acquisitive instinct. The great missionary Moravians established at Herrnhut a family community where each worked for Christ and for the good of all, transforming the Vale of baboons into the Rome of Grace. The Christian specialists in England and France, the priest-workers of present-day France, even the idealists of theoretical Marxist Communism at the start became, as Archbishop William Temple said, "a Christian heresy." It is a good thing that has gone bad, a dream of brotherhood which has become a nightmare through the perversion of men who try to base a brotherhood of men, while denying the Fatherhood of God through their adoption as sons through Christ the Elder Brother.

Second, to the undoubted need of community, the Church is meant to be God's answer. Listen to what representatives of three different centuries and three different religious traditions say about the nature of the Church. There is Cyprian, the dark North African bishop of the third century AD. "No man can have God as His father who has not the Church as his Mother." John Calvin, the greatest Reformed theologian writes in the sixteenth century: "What God has joined ought not to be divided and those to whom He himself is Father, the Church also is mother." (*Institutio* IV, i. 1, 4). John Wesley also affirms: "The New Testament knows nothing of solitary Christians." God has therefore willed this fellowship, transcending space and time, the centuries and the continents, as the communal expression of his love. By the same token he wills us in the name of Jesus Christ to overcome all the barriers to community.

The Word was made flesh, a message was enfleshed in the person of the eternal son of God, who perfectly exemplified the obedience which man owes to God and the forgiving love he owes to his brethren, and the saving, rescuing, caring for the souls, bodies and societies of men. The Gospel of God was enfleshed in the sacrificial and obedient life of our Lord. The Church is in the instrument of his continuing work, the Word of his Gospel in action, breaking down the walls of partition, integrating sin-broken personalities, and challenging the hatreds and disinterestedness that divide the communities of men. And he does it through the world-wide community that is the new race.

THE BARRIERS TO COMMUNITY

1. How Christ overcame the barriers of racial prejudice through Robert Moffat.

2. How Christ overcame the class barriers through the group of Christian Socialists in mid-19th century England, numbering Ludlow, Maurice, and Charles Kingsley as its doughtiest fighters. It was Kingsley, author of *The Water Babies*, a book not of fairy stories, but of propaganda against the use of boys as human chimney-brushes who wrote that religion was: "an opium-dose for keeping beasts of burden patient while they were being over-loaded." (*Politics for the People*, 53). Or, Keir Hardie, member of the

Evangelical Union, associated with Scottish Congregationalism, who was the founder of the modern Labor Party, and who believed in a Christianity which was, like Amos, prophetic and protested against social wrongs. He said, criticizing the rigid individualism of the orthodox of his day: "I am impatient with a religion which looks only to heaven in the next world, and ignores the hell in this." He turned *The Miner*, which he edited, into an advanced political journal. And this is Christian revolution, he proclaimed: "We need today a return to the principles of the Gospel which, by proclaiming all men sons of God and brethren one with another, makes it impossible for one, Shylock-like, to insist on his rights at the expense of another."

In 1893 he formed the Independent Labor Party (as distinct from the Fabian Society and the Social Democratic Federation). He said: "Socialism is a great moral movement. I am a socialist because socialism means fraternity founded on Justice." In 1892 he was returned as the first Socialist M.P. in history and he entered Parliament wearing a cloth cap, the badge of his devotion to his own underprivileged folk, representing West Ham. His first supporters actually pawned clocks and dinner cutlery and crockery to borrow money to print their handbills. The movement he espoused actually formed the government of England in 1924, within thirty years of the foundation of the Party.

PART TWO

Preaching in a World in Crisis
(South Africa)

17

The Rightful Claims of Heaven and Earth

Sermon Preached in South Africa

This reads as a testament on the relevance of the Church to Davies's beloved parish and to the religion department he founded. Saddened and under a cloud for preaching the brotherhood of all races, Davies is about to leave South Africa to return to England with his family. In a broad survey of the history of the Christian Church, he sees the shifts in its role from the religion of the poor, hoping for the Eternal City of justice, faith and charity, to the powerful Church of the age of faith, imposing laws, regulating science and creating educational art to depict the human and divine drama. Then, shattered by the concerns of the Renaissance and the age of Reason, which shifted the responsibility to the laity, the Christian Church lost its centrality and balance. Extreme reactions came about, like Pietism or Puritanism. Action and reaction abound in the history of Humanity as man has been torn between the transitory and the eternal, but the final message is that while living in the here and now, the human race needs to keep one eye on eternity.

- Hebrews 13:14: "For here have we no continuing City, but we seek one to come."

- Acts 21:39: "I am a Jew . . . a citizen of no mean city."

THIS TEXT HAS AN all too topical relevance, and even that may be misunderstood. In the temporal sense, our family is moving from the "City of the Saints" to the "Home of Lost Causes," which being very symbolically interpreted is a movement from Heaven to Hell. If it were literally interpreted, the prospect is even worse; for we move from the dazzling sunlight to the river mists, from plenty to austerity. And personally, if we may use technology as a category of interpretation, a cultural stockfish struggling in the pellucid pool becomes a sardine in the ocean.

But a sermon should not be an excuse for personal fancies. In saying farewell this evening from the pulpit of Trinity Church, before so many familiar faces of this Christian family, I want to take the vaster and much more important implications of this text.

My theme is: the rightful claims of heaven and earth—the rights of eternity and time.

The writer of the Epistle to the Hebrews lived at a time when Christians were a struggling minority in the vast Roman Empire. To be a Christian in his day was to be a despised member of a modern sect, held in contempt by the Judaism from which it sprang. He was considered as the fanciful upholder that a Galilean carpenter was the long-awaited revealer and redeemer of mankind who met his just fate on the Cross. It was also to belong to a raggle-taggle motley crew of the lower class, which the Roman citizens sneered at as working-class fanatics, and which the Greeks found a fascinating curiosity. The Church itself knew better. But its members had to be reminded that if they were harried and persecuted and sneered at—treated like low criminals—this was exactly the due of their Leader. Their consolation must be two-fold. Firstly, they were sharing in the sufferings of Christ; and secondly, they were preparing for life in a Celestial City where "the slings and arrows of outrageous fortune" could not touch them. "For we seek no lasting City, we seek the City to come."

Our situation is somewhat different. Civilization and Empire were the first sons of the Church. We are the heirs of the Khan centuries. In the long centuries of the Christian dispensation, in which our churches have proliferated round the globe, our laws have commended the justice that is due to men made in the image of God and redeemed in Christ. Our very science has been made possible because Christianity has dethroned the demons that the ancient superstitions made the world believe in. Our art and drama has grown out of the desire to perpetuate the loveliness of the divine artist and the significance of the divine drama of our Redemption. And now this precious asset of our life, this necessity is fast becoming a luxury. Renaissance man has overthrown Biblical Man and we live in the afterglow of the Christian civilization of the Middle Ages. Our forefathers in the faith could say: "We seek no lasting City." Now, we have to confess that the majority of men make their Credo: "We seek a lasting City, an earthly one."

Can we go back? No, there is no way backward in history. To rebuild the so-called ages of faith would be as foolish as to sell television sets and buy crystal-sets, to replace electric lights with the flickering grease of candles, to pull down our houses and creep back in skins under the overarching eaves of caves, to scrap Einstein and call back Copernicus from the grave. That is impossible but many intellectual and theological ostriches wish to bury their heads in the sands of oblivion.

If we cannot go back into history, may we not learn from it? I believe that we can and we must, from the succession of the Apostles and the succession of Judas. If the tragedy of yesterday, I mean the Middle Ages, was to subordinate the whole of life to heaven, to sacrifice the present for the future, the tragedy of the present is to eliminate the future City entirely for the sake of the Earthly City. Both are mistakes and we may learn from their errors.

To seek only the Heavenly City led to what are the errors of Quietism and Puritanism. Dr. John Baillie reminds us in his superb study *And the life everlasting* [1935] that a totalitarian claim for heaven leads to the neglect of the rightful claims of earth. To quote his words: "If the streets of the heavenly city were to be of shining gold and its walls of precious stone, then what matter though the streets of the earthly City were somewhat ill paved and the walls of the cottage were tumbling about our ears?" That was the attitude. "Sit down. O men of God," it argued, "His Kingdom He will bring." We want acquiescence, acceptance, not rebellion and revolution, and transformation of the conditions of society.

Today we hear from the narrow-minded citizens of the world's Bible Belts the same cry: "The Christian has no right to interfere with politics." But is it not the Bible itself in deep concern for social justice which exposes the smooth, slick words of a murderer: "Am I my brother's keeper?" You and I are our brother's keeper and the ballot-box is, conscientiously used, the sacrament of human brotherhood. If any man whatever the superficial pigmentation of his skin lives in a hovel, even if he is said to be content to do so, whether it be on the East Side of New York or in a Johannesburg ramshackle hut, he is the brother for whom Christ died. A Christian that forgets that and is not perpetually haunted by that sensitivity of conscience is a quietist perverter of the love of Christ universal in its scope. And his cry: "O it will be glory for me" is at once over-optimistic in view of the Judgment to come, and blinded from the truth by the false halo created by his own complacency.

The other result of too great a concern for the Celestial City is Puritanism, the excesses of which are found in all ages and in all Communions. Its characteristic weakness is the hardening of religion into a Pharisaic censoriousness ("I am better than you") and this ugliness of soul produces an ugly misrepresentation of the pleasures of life as all snares of the devil, arising from its denial that God made the world and found that it was good. It refuses to take seriously the fact that the Son of God was really incarnate in a human psycho-physical organism, a personality in a body.

Even choice souls were bound in its strait-jacket. John Bunyan threw away his flute because it was a distraction in his heavenly pilgrimage. Churches that had glorious representations of the mighty acts of God through his Son and his servants, the saints, [suffered] under the impulse of Puritanism, [that] smashed the stained-glass, white-washed the walls, banished the cross and threw the silver candles on the dust-heap; their women dressed in forbidding grey and their men wore hats that looked like church steeples: "Let us have no more of beauty; let us banish sex; let us throw away poetry, novels and drama and wine. Science is but idle curiosity . . . No more cakes and ale!" O what a loss was all this! The effects of the extreme iconoclasm of the Puritan wing of the Reformation are still around us. And, worst of all, the artists, the scientists, the poets, the musicians had to remain tone-deaf and color-blind and educationally frustrated if they were to stay with the Church. No wonder many left and that centuries of suspicion have still to be overcome and that a forward-looking minister is criticized as being both a modernist and a Roman Catholic if he claims art, music, science and liturgy for the enrichment of the Church of God.

Never again must we forget the prior claims of earth and it was, in the long perspective of history, worth even the losing of the provinces of Christendom that God should enable us to be on our guard against winning heaven at the cost of losing the loveliness of earth and the claims of social justice.

In the second place our dire danger today is that the ever-pressing claims of time shall blot out eternity. And our spirits were made so that earth will never satisfy them fully. Said Dr. Johnson: "Man like an animal has wants; but unlike an animal, he is never satisfied."

The tragedy of an exclusively this-worldly frame of reference is that it is utopian! It is over-optimistic. Against every blueprint for a transformed social order in this world the Christian writes three words, which are its condemnation: egotism, suffering and death. And these three words are like the winds of realism that blow down the house of cards that we call social planning. Do not misunderstand me! I believe that theology apart, there is no more important study than sociology. But, as one of the most distinguished of them, Dr. Karl Manheim of the London School of Economics, has asked: "Who is to plan the planners? And who is to rule our rulers? And the answer is God." Create your garden cities with national health schemes, free physicians and free psychiatrists. But who can minister to a mind that is morally diseased? Again, the answer is God. Bear suffering without bitterness. Build yourself escape hatches like the gigantic fraud that Evelyn Waugh has satirized in his novel about the Hollywood cemetery where all is a flowery conspiracy to hide the reality of death; but you cannot escape it even if you mitigate its effect upon the mourners by technically operated cheerful music, undertakers dressed like waiters at the Ritz, and canisters for the ashes of your beloved dead that look like caskets in which they have been presented with the freedom of the City of Oxford. The brute facts of man's individual and social egotism (sin), his suffering, physical and mental, and his lonely death cannot be dismissed. But, thanks be to God, they can be overcome. This is the victory: even our faith!

Spinoza, even in the pink of health, fortified by the complacency of regular meals and a satisfied paunch, declares: "The Free man thinks of nothing less than death; his wisdom is a meditation not upon death, but upon life." But St. Paul, always flirting with death in travel and persecution, peers into its hollow eye-sockets, as he exclaims: "The last enemy that shall be destroyed is death."

Three centuries later, the dispossessed and hunted Athanasius, well-named the deathless one, speaks for all Christians when he says:

> For as when a tyrant has been utterly vanquished by a true Emperor and is bound hand and foot, all who pass by jeer at him, smiting and abusing him, no longer fearing his rage and cruelty, because of the victorious Emperor; so also death, having been branded as infamous by the Savior on the Cross and bound hand and foot, all in Christ who pass through trample on it and, as witness to Christ,

deride death, scoffing at it and saving the words placarded above it: "Where Death is Thy Victory? Where Hades is Thy sting?"

Our solution, the acceptance of this tension is to be this-worldly and other-worldly; this-worldly without too deep an attachment which time cannot satisfy; other-worldly without a neglect of the duties and beauties of earth.

Let a devout Dutch monk, known as St. Thomas-a-Kempis, and an English poet, express this balance, without which we deify earth and depersonalize heaven. Says Thomas: "The sons of God, standing upon the things that are present, do contemplate the things that are eternal. They look on transitory things with the left eye and with the right do behold the things of Heaven."

Says Wordsworth, taking the lark as the symbol of the personality of man:

> Leave to the nightingale her shady wood;
> A privacy of glorious light is thine,
> Whence thou dost pour upon the world a flood
> Of harmony, with instinct more divine;
> Type of the wise, who soar but never roam—
> True to the kindred points of Heaven and Home.

Your addresses and ours are Oxford on the edge of eternity.

18

Resolutions: A New Year Sermon, 1950

Preached in South Africa

New Year's Day is a time to make vows, not just wishes, for a new beginning in the life with Christ, in remembrance of and gratitude for his flesh torn and his blood spilled for the love of mankind, as in the Communion Service. Memento mori. There is no postponing: these vows must be made in public, with the help of the Christian community. Yet Davies also makes allowance for private vows, emerging from the shattering experiences that seed the souls of individuals like Lincoln or Shaftesbury, and slowly burgeoning, eventually come to full bloom when those individuals gain access to power and are able to impose their insight on public policy.

- Psalm 116:18: "I will pay my vows unto the LORD now in the presence of all his people."

THE NEW YEAR, SAYS the cynic, is the time when we make vows that we don't intend to keep. Are we then not to make vows or resolutions? What would you think of a man who refused to enter the recent speed boat regatta in East London because he thought he couldn't win a prize? Or, of a man who decided to enter the Civil Service because he was afraid of the risks of private enterprise in business? God forbid that we should start the New Year by being complacent cowards—content to do less than the miserable little we did for Christ last year.

How then, should a Christian begin the New Year? The answer is by a new beginning of the life with God. The thoughts of Christmas centre on a new beginning that God made with a new baby: his Eternal Son. And God wants a new beginning as our response.

The text tells us how to make it: "I will pay my vows to the Lord now in the presence of all his people." I want you to notice the four important things our text is saying:

1. It speaks of *vows*, not airy resolutions, but personal promises. We speak of taking the marriage vows, of the solemn personal promises made by bride and bridegroom to each other: "I take thee to be my lawful wedded wife or husband to have and to hold for better for worse, for richer for poorer, in sickness or in health, until death us do part." Could anything be more solemn? Yes, the marriage of Christ to the Church. It is taken not only for life but for eternity. Death never shall part Christ and his beloved. This is the spirit in which tonight we are to renew our Covenant.

2. The text also speaks of making vows to the right *person*, to the Lord. The strongest vows are those made in love. And have we not visible and tangible proofs of our Lord's love before us tonight? The red wine is an effectual reminder of the precious blood outpoured from the Cross for us undeserving men. The broken bread speaks of the broken body of Jesus and his wounds, like torn mouths, proclaiming his never-ending love. Of course, we shall make this promise of loyalty. He loved me and gave himself for me. This is not a vacillating resolution we make, but a covenant—to be God's men and women this year, to fight as our parents promised at our baptism, manfully, under the banner of Christ's Cross.

3. We make the vows at *the right time*. We make them *now*. We do not know how many of us in the mercy of God will be alive and here, twelve months from now. In the midst of life we are in death. God calls whom he wills and when he wills. Richard Baxter used to address his letters in these words: "From Kidderminster at the door of Eternity." We are at East London, at the door of Eternity. The Catholics have a proverb about the last minute mercies of God: "Betwixt the stirrup and the ground / He something sought and something found"(Graham Greene: *Brighton Rock*). That is, they believe that deathbed repentance enables a man to find God and God to discover Him. God's mercies are marvelous. But we should be fools to presume upon them. What a miserable and mean idea, that we should leave God as it were the cigarette-ends of our life. We first train for our career, we next give the best to our family; we settle our own security and make our pile; and then God comes as the afterthought. Yet, that is exactly what many Christians are doing. I plead with you tonight: *now* is the acceptable time. God wants you in the fullness of your

manhood and your womanhood. He would make your resolutions, your sacred promises, your covenant . . . be renewed tonight.

4. Fourthly, the text urges us to make our vows in the right place, in the *Church*. What is a vow must be a public vow. The solitary vow is a feeble vow. This may be illustrated by a naturalist's narrative.

He recounts that one day beside the great St. Lawrence River, overlooking a waterfall, he saw the gradually freezing river bear on its icy waters the carcass of a sheep. Suddenly a vulture swooped like a thunderbolt from the heavens and thrust its fierce talons into the cold flesh of the sheep. Greedily, it tore the meat, and greedily, consumed it. Slowly, the river approached the waterfalls, and the bird, despite its hunger, had not lost its alertness, thinking that when the waterfall was imminent, it could fly off and let the rest of the mauled carcass plunge to the depths, whilst it soared aloft. On went the carcass and the bird, but when the moment came for flight, its talons had frozen hard to the carcass. Frantically, it tried to dislodge itself; but in vain. At the swirling waters at the foot of the waterfall there were soon two carcasses, not one.

So too, man, in the greedy grip of sin, gives his destiny a thought now and then. But as long as he postpones the day of decision, he is tied to his worst self. Struggle as he may, he can only cry out with St. Paul: "O who will deliver me from the body of this death?"

My friends, you cannot pull yourself up by your own bootlaces. The good news of the Gospel is that God will lift you! And the congregation of God's people—the friends of Christ—are here to light you. Make your vows, not like a Robinson Crusoe, stranded from your friends, on an island, but together with the fighters for God.

The Church exists to be your helper. It is the army of the living God, not a set of isolated guerilla fighters in lone engagements.

Moreover the Gospel is not that God helps those who help themselves; but, [in the words of Shirley Bassey]: "Help of the Helpless, O abide with me." God sent his Son into the front line to be the Captain of our salvation. It is faith, absolute trust and loyalty to him, that gives us the victory.

You say: "What is the use of a vow made by one person?" Abraham Lincoln as a youth, watched a Negro slave being put up for auction and saw his prospective master thrash him—merely to test how docile he was. This burned into his soul and he vowed that if ever he had power, he would strike out this evil thing. To accomplish his vow, he was prepared for Civil War. And so one man's vow cleared the world of slavery!

Lord Shaftesbury was in London on holiday from Eton School. One day wandering down the East End of the capital city he saw a pauper's funeral, the pall-bearers were drunk, and as they lurched round the corner, the body fell out of the coffin. He was sickened, though a boy.

Later, he found mill-boys, sleeping under the arches of bridges or on the tops of deserted factories. He swore that he would use all his inheritance to secure a deal more just for the underprivileged, homes for the poor, properly regulated working hours for youths, and this vow made him a social reformer.

Your view need not be a dramatic one, but your life in 1950 is not to be spiritually a wasted year. You will begin it at Christ's table with all of us. And, before you receive the nourishment of faith, you will say: "Father I have sinned before heaven and before thee and I am not worthy to be called Thy son or daughter. Make me as one of thy hired servants. O Christ, forgive the wasted years. Help me, O help me, to be a Disciple, not a mocker."

"I will pay my vows unto the Lord now in the presence of all his people." Thus will you guarantee true happiness throughout 1950, and God will see that it is a very Happy New Year to you all.

19

Race-Tensions in South Africa

Formative Factors and Suggested Solutions

This lecture attempts to show the complexity of the situation in South Africa, in order to expand on some of the simplistic views held by the uninformed: reducing the race struggle to black and white, whilst the land is peopled with other races, or reducing consideration of foreign presence to only the Dutch and the British. The lecture ends on the options open to the government of South Africa: total assimilation, total separation, or Christian rule, whilst considering the even greater complicatons of economic and sociological factors.

"MORAL LEPERS" IS PROBABLY the phrase which, in the judgment of thinking and conscientious persons in Europe, evaluates the White population and their racial attitudes in Southern Africa. That this evaluation is no journalistic exaggeration may be gathered from two quotations, one from an ecclesiastical historian of world renown, and the other from an English bishop. Professor K. S. Latourette writes:

> The Whites were determined to remain in control, politically, economically and socially. The result was discrimination and acute and chronic inter-racial tension which, next to the anti-Semitism of the Third German Reich, were the most serious on the planet.[1]

The Bishop of Bristol's reference to South Africa is all the more significant because it is merely incidental:

> It is hardly an exaggeration to say that if we were to take religious division as we find it at its sharpest, say between Catholic and Protestant in Northern Ireland, and racial division as we find it at

---

1. Latourette, K. S., *A History of the Expansion of Christianity*, VII, 225.

its sharpest, say between Black and White in South Africa, and mix them both together, we should get something like the equivalent of the situation which confronted Paul in the eastern half of the Roman Empire.[2]

White South Africans are, therefore, branded as moral pariahs. Now the aim of this essay is neither to "white-wash" the situation (in either sense of that term), nor to agree with the evaluation. It seeks rather to understand how the situation of acute inter-racial tension arose and to explore the varied solutions which have been advanced for the settlement of a grave and growing problem.

1. The first feature of the color-problem in South Africa is its remarkable *complexity*. The problem is not merely how to enable Blacks and Whites to live together in peace in the country. There are, in fact, four main racial groups in the Union, each with several sub-divisions. The four divisions may be called, for convenience: 1. Europeans: including persons of Dutch and British extraction and others, of French, German, Scandinavian and Jewish stock; 2. Asiatics: including Indians and Chinese; 3. Coloreds, persons of mixed blood, primarily Eurafricans (the products of miscegenation between White and Black) with a considerable number of Malayan extraction; and 4. Natives, that is, persons of native stock. Thus it will readily be seen that South Africa resembles an anthropological zoo.

This in itself would make for racial difficulties, but the acuteness of the tensions is due to the attempt of the White minority to dominate the non-White majority. If the ruthlessness of the domineering develops in exact proportion to the increase of fear, then each census is a greater nightmare to the insecure Whites. In 1946, the numbers of the different racial groups were as follows: Europeans, 2,335,460; Asiatics, 282,539; Mixed and other Coloreds, 905,090; and Natives, 7,735,809, with a total population of 11,258,858. The tension is caused by the fact that the Europeans (approximately one in five of the total population), whilst the Africans constitute 68.7 per cent. The half-castes, as the Coloreds would be termed elsewhere, are 8 per cent and the Asiatics 2.5 per cent of the population. The problem was already acute enough between Boers, Britons and the Bantus in the early nineteenth century, but it was greatly intensified by the importation of Indians as sugar-laborers in Natal in the later part of the century, and of Chinese for the goldmines in the early twentieth

---

2. Cockin, F. A., *The Holy Spirit and the Church*, 1939, 67.

century.[3] All these racial groups regard South Africa as their home and their families have been settled here for many generations in most cases, and for two centuries or more in the cases of the Dutch speaking South Africans and the Bantu.

A further complication arises in the differing outlooks of the two major European groups, respectively those of Dutch and British stock. It would be inaccurate to state baldly that the former are much less liberal in race attitudes than the latter, yet the Afrikaner has cut off his roots from Holland and is more integrated in the life and history of South Africa. The cynic might say that the Englishman still regards England as home, and if his more liberal race attitude jeopardizes European dominance, he can always return home. The Afrikaner, who is in the majority amongst Europeans, has cut the painter tying him to the quay of Europe and knows no other land.

Thus a great variety of races, languages and cultures complicates the social pattern in the Union and the vast numerical superiority of the non-Europeans over the Europeans provides the fear which interprets might as right and assumes reconciliation to be weakness.

2. We must next ask: What factors have formed this acute inter-racial tension in South Africa? It is indeed difficult to analyze so complex an attitude as racial superiority on the part of the dominant group, but the outstanding factors may be isolated as historical, economic, political and social.

For the present our concern will be the *historical* factor.[4]

Mr. Bernard Shaw has stated that the trouble with South Africans is that they will keep on fighting the Anglo-Boer War. One of the tragedies of race-relations is that White South Africans keep on fighting the Kaffir Wars of the nineteenth century and earlier. It is impossible to understand the mental make-up of the contemporary South African White unless one realizes that his is an inherited "frontier-attitude." European settlement began in South Africa in 1652 when Commander van Riebeeck was ordered by the East India Company to establish a victualling-station at the Cape as a half-way house between the Netherlands and the Netherland

---

3. Hellmann E., ed. *Handbook on Race Relations in South Africa*, 1949, 6.

4. The reader should consult Professor I. D. MacCrone's admirable monograph, *Race attitudes in South Africa* (an historical, experimental and psychological study). Oxford, 1937.

East Indies. From the first, White men have held two attitudes towards their Black neighbors: first, they regarded them as a menace to white security and secondly as innately inferior.

These attitudes have been strengthened by three centuries of almost unremitting warfare between White and Black for the possession of the land. South Africa's lack of water for a long time forced its inhabitants, even when farmers, to be militant nomads. Van Riebeeck's men found the neighboring Hottentots to be incorrigible cattle-thieves. The Dutch farmers and the English Settlers of 1820 found the foraging Bantu a menace to their crops and their lives. It is significant that when Piet Retief, the leader of the Voortrekkers, left Grahamstown, then the English Settlers' City, for the hinterland, the citizens sped him on his way with a Bible and completely shared in this Dutchman's disapproval of the British Government's policy in freeing slaves and therefore manumitting their cheap labor.

As for the White's sense of racial superiority, it had a two-fold origin. He argued naively that the military conqueror who had wrested the land from the natives was evidently superior. He also affirmed that the Blacks were inferior because they were heathen, whereas he, a Calvinist, belonged to the company of God's elect. Sometimes this narrow and dogmatic Dutch Calvinism became no more than a Biblical rationalization of the *status quo*. Even a nineteenth-century Dutch, Commissary Janssens, who was sympathetic to the work of Dr. van der Kemp (first missionary to the Bantu and sent by the London Missionary Society), can write of the Hottentots at Bethelsdorp:

> They call themselves men and Christians, the Kaffirs and Hottentots heathen, and for this reason they believe they are permitted everything. A brother of Thomas Ferreira . . . has made the discovery that the Hottentots are the descendants of the cursed race of Ham, and consequently are condemned by God Almighty to servitude and ill-treatment.[5]

This example of Old Testament exegesis has supplied many a Dutch *predikant* with a convenient text in the past, though to-day it is worn rather threadbare.

But, more significant for the understanding of the White South African, is the historical role of the Black man as the formidable and treacherous foe brought to his knees by [the White man's] great ancestors,

---

5. MacCrone, I. D., *Op. cit.*, 130.

the 1820 Settlers and the Voortrekkers. The school text-books in history leave little to the imagination in refurbishing the events that demonstrate the black heart of the native. One of the red-letter days of the Union's calendar is a public holiday known as "Dingaan's Day." This celebrates the massacre of Retief and his Voortrekkers by the Zulu chief, Dingaan. Another favorite event for national recollection is the Slagter's Nek Rebellion, an incident in which Hottentot soldiers sent to arrest the Dutch rebel Bezuidenhout on a charge of cruelty to a Hottentot servant were fired upon by the Dutchman, who was eventually killed by their returning fire. This incident is still used by unscrupulous politicians to fire the fuse of anti-British and anti-Bantu feeling. Bezuidenhout has thus become a martyr in Afrikaner hagiology. Such events keep, not evergreen, but ever-red the memory of racial antagonism. South Africans will not let bygones be bygones. History is thus a record of the triumphs of the *Herrenvolk!*

3. The *economic* factor is equally as significant as the historical in the determination of race relationships. With this is allied the problem of the virtual failure of the Socialists in South African politics. Traditionally Socialism, with the backing of the trade unions, has been the champion of the underprivileged classes in Europe. In South Africa the Black folk comprise the proletariat and it might be expected that the seeds of Socialism would have found secure lodgment in them. That it has not done so is due to two factors: first, there is no direct representation of any non-European group in the parliamentary constitution; secondly, many trade unions have introduced the color-bar as a safeguard for the White members. In addition, of recent years the Government has refused to recognize any trade union as a registered union if it included non-Europeans in its membership. Some unions, such as the typographical, sweet and food-canning workers, have retaliated by organizing Africans into their own separate unions. Most African unions, however, have been organized independently because of their different interests.

The comments of Dr. H. J. Simons are illuminating in this context:

> The close association that exists in Great Britain and continental countries between trade-unions and working-class political parties is not a feature of the movement in South Africa. Some unions have formal connections with the Labor Party, but racial and nationalist dissensions are too pronounced for such a relationship to become widespread. The Labor Party, having its attention

focused on parliamentary action, makes no bid for the support of the disenfranchised non-Europeans who tend to adhere to the Communist Party and to organizations such as the Natal Indian Congress and African National Congress.[6]

It is important to observe that economic fears mitigate against the training of Africans as skilled workers. It is believed by the impartial observer that such an attitude produces the following prejudicial results: it prevents the full use of the greatest resources of the country—the eight million African workers; this, as a consequence, prevents any considerable increase in the national income; and that prevents any appreciable improvement in the standardization of housing, health services and social services. Furthermore, a skilled African proletariat would have greater purchasing power and provide a ready home market for the increased production. Once more, the improvement in African health would react favorably on the health of the European population, whose children are cared for and whose meals are prepared by native and colored domestic servants. Microbes recognize no color-bar! The man who opposes the provision of opportunities for Africans to learn skilled trades is thus cutting off his nose to spite his white face.

Behind the economic factor there is the gaunt face of fear. In this field, too, faith would prove more far-sighted than the so-called "realistic" attitude of discrimination. Furthermore, the refusal of the African's right to participate equally with the European in trade unions is driving him into the welcoming arms of the Communist Party. And this, in turn, argues only a short-term security for the White minority now in power. The self-appointed "defenders of White civilization" are proving to be its wreckers, for no society can rest firmly on the fissures of economic injustice.

4. The *social* and *political* factors in the racial situation may be dealt with more briefly. Equally with the historical and economic factors they are the products of fear. Since the determining factor in South African life is the skin pigmentation (or, strictly, the lack of it), no opportunity for miscegenation must be allowed, for this is disrespect for the purity of the White blood, and mixing of the White race would imply equality which spells the doom of White domination. The same results would follow if the non-Europeans were enfranchised. The White minority vastly out-numbered by the non-Europeans claims that it cannot afford either social or political

---

6. Hellmann E., ed., *op. cit.* 169.

egalitarianism. This fear is not, of course, entirely irrational because it is the recognition that past repression would clamor for vengeance when the non-Europeans can outvote the Europeans. Nonetheless, to postpone the ending of repression is also only to postpone the social Day of Judgment. The possibility that the White man might act as the political, economic and educational trustee of the Black man is not regarded as a realistic possibility, apart from the views of such distinguished Liberals as the late Deputy Prime Minister, the Hon. J. H. Hofmeyr.

We may conclude our all too rapid survey of the ingredients of race prejudice by asking a sociological question: what functions are served by the racial attitude of the dominant White minority?

In the first place, this attitude is an integrating factor that helps to preserve the identity of the White group, making it conscious of being a small white island in a black sea. Thus the ranks are closed against the common enemy. The cement of the whited sepulcher is fear.

The second function of the group attitude of the Whites is to provide historical continuity and a consequent sense of security. This feeling of group continuity is strengthened by the recollection of victories over the Black enemy in the past. The White sagas of yesterday thus breed confidence in the present.

Thirdly, the attitude of dominating the native provides a ready criterion of group membership. Therefore, hostility towards the native is expected on the part of White persons and this demonstrates the group identity, apart from providing a safety-valve through which hostilities which might arise within the group are projected outside it.

Fourthly, class and economic motives are subserved by the group attitude, by insisting that the color-line shall be the same as the horizontal division in the economic and political structures of South African society. The group attitude thus ensures that the Black man's ceiling shall be the White man's basement.

Finally, the rigid group attitude enables individual members on joining the group to make an easy conventional adjustment to the natives and thus prevent any disruption of the group for reasons of sentiment or sympathy.[7]

These functional factors indicate the tenacity with which the White group clings to its color prejudices. Possibly only a greater fear will ulti-

---

7. These functional factors are admirably analyzed by MacCrone, *op. cit.* 254 f.

mately drive out the present fears which place a premium on a policy of repression.

5. The time has now come to consider the various *solutions* which have been put forward to resolve the acute inter-racial tensions in the Union of South Africa.[8] There are five fairly clearly distinguished racial policies which emerge from amongst a number of entirely unsatisfactory or merely ephemeral suggestions.

The first to be considered is *Total Assimilation*. This means the entire physical, social and political fusion of the races in order to eliminate the racial conflict. Such a policy would require the removal of discrimination in residential areas, educational institutions, trades and professions. A further necessity would be direct political representation for adult members of every race. An inevitable consequence of such a policy would be inter-racial marriage. To some degree the rapid urbanization of the natives is already producing cultural and economic assimilation by imitation of the Europeans. Amongst wealthier Africans and poorer Whites there is probably some miscegenation, but this is not likely to be high because this is generally as distasteful a prospect for the non-European as for the European. In many ways such a policy would seem to be the likeliest to lead to complete elimination of racial prejudice. If all races were equally mixed, no member of any race could claim racial superiority. The end of all pure races in South Africa would also be the end of a pigmentation superiority-complex. The solution is, however, open to a serious practical objection. It would be met by the most fanatical opposition on the part of the Europeans and would lead to an immediate worsening of relationships already gravely strained. It cannot, with the present yawning cultural chasm dividing the average White from the average Black, be regarded as a practical solution to the problem.

A second suggested solution is *Parallelism*. It means, in brief, differentiation without territorial segregation. Its most distinguished exponent, Lord Lugar, defined it in the following terms:

> ... complete uniformity in ideas; absolute equality in the paths of knowledge and culture, equal opportunities for those who strive ... in matters social and racial a separate faith, each pursuing his

---

8. Cf. Quintin Whyte: *Apartheid and other Policies*. South African Institute of Race Relations: Johannesburg, 1948.

own race purity and race pride; equally in things spiritual, agreed divergence in the physical and material.[9]

Put concretely, this means that each race would have separate but equally advantageous provisions in the way of schools, churches, clubs, health facilities and occupational opportunities. This idealistic policy aims at inter-racial justice and for that reason it was sponsored by Dr. J. H. Oldham. Nonetheless, the objection to this and to all other forms of segregation is that it is too costly and too late. It is too late because the African is already integrated in European industry and thoroughly detribalized; it is too costly because it would mean replacing cheap native labor by dearer White labor. Moreover, it is extremely unlikely that White South Africans would agree to part with their underpaid native boys and women as domestic servants. A leisured class is not likely to take up tasks which it has hitherto regarded as menial and manual "Kaffir jobs."

The third cure put forward is *Total Segregation*. This would involve the removal of the entire African population to native reserves and the creation of a "Bantustan" on the analogy of Pakistan. Its avowed aim is to make the non-Europeans economically, socially and politically independent. Logically, this policy should also require the setting up of autonomous states for each racial group, thus creating separate European, African, Colored and Indian states, each maintaining its racial purity and developing its own culture. The advantages of such a policy, it is argued, are that it would prevent any clash of racial interests and the production of a "fake" European culture by non-Europeans, whilst being based upon a Christian sense of justice. The main difficulties are financial and temporal. It would take considerable time both to train the non-Europeans to manage their own affairs and to recruit Europeans to take the place of non-Europeans in industry and commerce. Furthermore, European capital would have to be diverted to finance non-European autonomous states at the very time that it would be required for the stabilization of European economy. The practical objections raised against parallelism would also apply to this policy.

The fourth solution advocated is *Apartheid*, or Partial Segregation. This, a variant of the third policy, is the most popular policy and the Nationalist Party became the Government of the Union on this very platform. It is also a policy strongly supported by the three Dutch Reformed

---

9. *Dual Mandate*, 1929.

Churches, the membership of which constitutes the majority of the European population. The importance of this policy, therefore, can hardly be overemphasized in terms of its influence. It can be most impartially described by a summary of the findings of the Nationalist Party which was presented by Dr. D. F. Malan, the present Prime Minister. He stated that the Nationalist Party

> wants to give the non-European races the opportunity to develop in their own spheres, according to their natural capacity and adaptability, and wants to assure for them fair and just treatment in the administration of the country: but the Party is vigorously opposed to any mixture of blood between the European and non-European races. The Party declares itself to be in favor of territorial and political segregation of the Native as well as of separation of European and non-European in general and, as far as practical, also in the residential sphere. Furthermore, the Party wants to [protect] all sections of the community against Asiatic immigration and "concurrence" among other things, by preventing further intrusion into their sphere of life, as well as by a conscious plan for Asiatic immigration.[10]

This policy appears to be inspired by motives of justice and this undoubtedly accounts for its adoption by the Dutch Reformed Churches, which, it should be remembered, have a remarkable record for missionary giving for enterprises outside as well as within the Union. On mature consideration, however, *Apartheid* appears to be but another mask for domination. It does not propose to give non-Europeans any political rights in the constitution, or even to permit Africans to organize their own trade unions. Even the education to be given to the Africans will (in a sinister phrase) attempt "to anchor them to their way of life." Some concessions are to be made to the Coloreds (for it seems that the Nationalists regard them with a favorable eye, which may be the expression of the guilty conscience of a race!) They will be represented in Parliament on a communal basis and a Cabinet Minister may be set aside with a Portfolio for Colored Affairs. The Indians receive rougher treatment, being regarded as an inassimilable element and the Party recommends that they should be repatriated regardless of cost. The most radical criticism of *Apartheid*, however, differently interpreted by some of its idealistic supporters, is that it would almost inevitably involve a subordination of the non-European

---

10. *Rand Daily Mail.* March 26, 1948. *Cf.* Hellerman, *op. cit.*, 530.

to the European, and that would be the rankest injustice. Furthermore, it is economically impracticable.

The fifth and last of the suggested solutions is *Christian Trusteeship*. This is associated with the name of the distinguished liberal statesman, the late J. H. Hofmeyr. In his Hoernlé Memorial Lecture of 1945, he claimed that the only possible basis was a Christian foundation, *if* race policies were to be equitable. This he described as follows:

> The central truth is that of the Fatherhood of God, carrying with it the implication of the brotherhood of man, irrespective of race or color or creed and a concept of a world-wide family, all the members of which stand in the same relationship.[11]

From the idealistic basis he urged the right of all men to develop their personalities, irrespective of racial origin. This involved for the trustees (the Europeans in South Africa) making provision of the fullest facilities for the non-European peoples both in their Reserves and in all parts of the country where they reside. For the wards (the non-Europeans) the policy means the acceptance of a period of tutelage and progressive development until they have reached their majority and can take their full part in affairs sharing responsibility with the trustees on an equal basis. The policy has been criticized as vague, but its exponents can retort that it is realistic because it does not involve the economic difficulties inevitable in any segregationist policy, whilst it does not advocate assimilation which the Europeans are not even prepared to consider. It has the further advantage of being in line with the trends of economics and the liberal policies of the British Protectorates and dependencies elsewhere in the Continent. Its hope is based upon "development." The real question which still remains is whether the policy would be implemented rapidly enough to meet non-European rising demands, or whether it might become an attempt to postpone still further the attainment of non-European citizenship.

6. What, then, may we hope for the future? It will be encouraging to consider some signs of promise in the contemporary scene. Apart from the pressure of world opinion, which is becoming increasingly sensitive to social and racial injustice, the chief grounds for hope are these: liberal statesmen and leaders of public opinion in South Africa; the work of the

---

11. *Christian Principles and Race Problems*. 1945.

Christian Churches (especially those which are missionary-minded); the work of the Institute of Race Relations; and the expansion of non-European education itself. The outstanding leader of liberal opinion in South Africa was undoubtedly the late J. H. Hofmeyr, whose fairly recent death was probably a greater loss to the non-Europeans than to his own race. In politics the Hofmeyr tradition lives on in two able and courageous champions of the non-Europeans. In the House of Assembly, Mrs. Margaret Ballinger, M.P. combines a deep knowledge of non-European living conditions with a high dialectical ability and Christian courage, whilst in the Senate, Dr. Edgar Brooks (formerly a professor of Politics and later the principal of Adams Mission College for Zulus) incarnates the sympathy and intrepidity of true liberalism. It is a significant tribute to Anglicanism that both of these legislators are communicants of the Church of the Province of South Africa. Perhaps the most colorful champion of non-Europeans on the South Africa scene, certainly the most well-known, the Rev. Michael Scott, is a priest of the same Communion. Alan Paton (author of *Cry, the Beloved Country*) is the outstanding representative of a number of liberal writers in South Africa.

Many of the doughtiest opponents of racial discrimination in the Union are the leaders of the Churches, particularly the English-speaking Churches. The bench of Anglican bishops is certainly no synonym for compromising timidity! Some Churches, notably the Anglican and Roman Catholic Churches, admit all races to their services and other Churches admit non-Europeans to their supreme Courts and Assemblies. The Congregationalists have perhaps gone the furthest in recent years in the direction of complete Christian color-blindness in electing a colored minister to be the chairman of the Congregational Union of South Africa.

The Churches are proving their liberalism in practice by their remarkable contribution to the up-building of African health and education on mission stations. It was estimated in 1935, for instance, that the Churches paid 13 per cent of the entire cost of African education. For this reason their leaders are sometimes hurt by wholesale British condemnation of race relationships in South Africa, feeling that Britain sometimes forgets her friends.

A most important contribution to the alleviation of race-tensions is being made by the South African Institute of Race Relations. This was founded in 1929 and is under the Directorship of Mr. Quintin Whyte, who succeeded Dr. Rheinallt Jones in this important post. This is a non-political fact-finding organization which is slowly but surely bringing the catalyst of science to bear on the hard crust of racial prejudice by creating a well-informed public opinion. It is enlisting the support of anthropologists, lawyers and the non-European leaders themselves for this task. A tribute must also be paid to the Jewish community for their support of the Institute. Under the influence of the Institute, joint European and African Councils have been formed in most of the leading cities and towns of the Union, which provide opportunities for Europeans and Africans to discuss common problems in an atmosphere of mutual trust.

Hopeful as these straws in the wind are, the most promising sign is to be found in the field of non-European education. The Government is increasing its subsidy for non-European education each year. For example, the total expenditure by the State in millions of pounds on African education was 0.1 in 1910, 0.3 in 1920, 0.6 in 1930, 1.0 in 1940 and 2.3 in 1945. Furthermore, 2.2 millions of pounds were spent on the subsidization of Colored and Indian education in 1945. While the figures do not compare well with the Government expenditure of 16.5 millions of pounds on European education in 1945, they do indicate a growing responsibility for non-European education.[12] In addition, more is spent per capita on non-European education by the Union Government than in any other British territory in Africa.

Higher education amongst non-Europeans has reached a more advanced stage in South Africa than in any other part of the Continent. In 1916, under the guidance of Dr Alexander Kerr, the South African Native College was founded at Fort Hare in the Eastern Cape. This was the first situation for the higher education of the non-Europeans to be established in South Africa. In 1946 it was preparing 324 students for the degrees of the University of South Africa, to which institution it was affiliated. Of these 260 were Africans, 35 Coloreds and 29 Indians. The fine residential hostels at Fort Hare have been built by the contributions of the Anglican, Methodist and Presbyterian Churches of South Africa. When in 1951 Rhodes University College attains to independent status as a University of its own right, Fort Hare will become a University College of this new University. Non-European students have also been admitted for some years the Universities of Cape Town and Witwatersrand, though the pres-

---

12. Hellmann, *op.cit.*, 383.

ent government has hinted that such facilities for non-Europeans may be withdrawn in the interests of its segregation policy. The University of Natal has an important non-European University College at Durban and is making provision for a non-European medical faculty. In Pretoria, the Dutch Reformed Churches have collaborated recently to found a small university institution for Africans. Furthermore, many of the Churches have established admirable educational institutions for non-Europeans, including teacher-training and industrial institutions. The most renowned are Lovedale (Presbyterian), Healdtown (Methodist), Adams College (American Congregationalist), Tiger Kloof (English Congregationalist), Mariannhill (Roman Catholic) and St. Matthew's, Keiskama Hoek (Anglican). Education, especially under Christian auspices, will give the non-European the opportunity to prove that he is no whit inferior in intelligence or cultural capacity than the European. Its value is being realized all the more as the thinking South African sees that repression breeds Communism amongst the underprivileged. The total situation, especially to those in the thick of it, may seem depressingly crepuscular, but light increases in intensity in this dark sub-Continent.

The Rev. Professor HORTON DAVIES, D.Phil. (Oxon.), D.D. (S. Africa)
Head of the Department of Divinity
in Rhodes University College at Grahamstown, South Africa

First published in Spinks, Stephens, editor. *The Hibbert Journal. A Quarterly Review of Religion, Theology, and Philosophy*. XLIX. London: Allen and Unwin, Jan. 1951. 118–27.

20

Resurgam

Preached on Remembrance Day at St. Andrews College Chapel in Grahamstown, South Africa

This sermon links three continents, England and South Africa, via two churches named after St. Andrews, one in Plymouth, England and the other in Grahamstown and England and America, via the towns of Plymouth and their great sea-farers. It is a call to courage and creativity in the midst of the shedding of blood, the spreading of fire and of devastation, ensuing from war, greed, and racism; it is a call to hope, to a change of hearts and the pursuit of life beyond destruction.

❧ Matthew 27:63: "After three days, I will rise again."

IN THE CENTER OF war-shattered Plymouth there is a church famous throughout the west of England. Like your own college, it is named St. Andrews in honor of the fisher-saint and patron of missionaries. This Church is proud to boast that the great admirals of England—Drake, Howard of Effingham and Blake—when their ships put in to Plymouth harbor, worshipped here. It is also proud to recall that the Pilgrim Fathers gathered there to renew their solemn promises and covenant to God and to each other, before setting out in the frail *Mayflower* to cross the Atlantic, and establish New England.

In the devastating raids of Plymouth, St. Andrews, like many other churches, was burned to the ground. Only the stone-walls, their grey blackened by fire, remained. The fine embossed roof and the splendid stained glass windows, with a hundred rare dyes shining in the evening sunlight, were merely a charred chaos.

But the vicar and his people determined to make the best of things. They did two things that caught the imagination of the citizens of Plymouth. They turned the wilderness of charred timber and fused glass into a garden, so that city people tired or depressed might rest their eyes on the newly springing grass and be cheered by the rich red of the geraniums they planted there. They did something else, which was even more important: they took a stone slab from the ruins and chiseled out of it the one word *RESURGAM*, and they placed this stone symbol high on a charred wall where all the passers-by could see it. The motto means: "I shall rise again." And it was the symbol of the people of Plymouth. I understand that this word is to be included in the new coat of arms of the ancient city of Plymouth.

This word *RESURGAM* stands for part of my text. After three days, I *will rise again*. Christianity, our holy faith, is based upon the fulfillment of that glorious promise. When Jesus died, cold-blooded Pontius Pilate, the fickle crowd who, within a week, had shouted: "Hail King," and: "Crucify Him," and the scheming priests of Judaism, all thought that they had finished with Jesus; and the disciples, like Peter, were going home again to their fishing. That was to have been the end of Christianity because it was to have been the end of Jesus. But he confounded them all by rising again from his grave and by returning from the frontiers of death. Before his coming, men believed that death was a cul-de-sac. He proved that for those who serve him, death is a tunnel, a leap into the dark and out into the light of eternity again.

This is Remembrance Day and it is fitting to remember that Christians are able to make the supreme sacrifice, believing that "he who loseth his life shall save it." Christ and his own shall conquer death, for death is swallowed up in victory. The noble are lost to the world, only to find themselves in heaven with God. "I will rise again," and they shall rise again.

I like the story of the Canadian officer during the Second World War who had joined up at the same time as his greatest friend. They were posted in the same company and went into the front line as comrades. This officer had the shattering experience of seeing his friend literally blown to smithereens by a shell beside him. He stopped for a moment, speechless, and then the words came, with quiet conviction: "It will take more than that to stop God." This was the Resurrection faith.

And because we have been called by God to share not only this life but all eternity with him, we must live the life eternal here and now. *Resurgam* must be our motto. Like a boxer defeated again and again by difficulties or temptations, we shall refuse to take the count, but get up again, and rise again. Jesus Christ, the Captain of our salvation, does not want milk-sops but boys and men who are courageous, generous, gentlemanly, called to live with the heroes and the greatest of heroes, our Lord, as his gallant soldiers. His promise is: "If I live, ye shall live."

I see in the words of our Lord a promise for his Church—the Church which is his Body. "I shall rise again." I am sure that our Lord is ambitious that boys of St. Andrews College should share in the rebirth and resurrection of his Church.

There are hospitals, clinics, and social service centers in plenty in South Africa, as there are schools, colleges and universities to care for the bodies and the minds of men; but Christ wants our everlasting souls to be cared for! That is the work of his Church—to give new life to dying souls. What is the use of saving a man's body from the tortures of disease, and making the blood to course again through his veins, if his soul is dead; you are resurrecting a body, and turning it into an animated corpse.

Christendom today is rotting because its men and women are filling their paunches and pockets, and letting their souls suffocate and their conscience become cancerous. What shall it profit a man, Briton, Boer or Bantu, if he gain the whole world and loses his own soul? The wilderness of human relationships and the deserts of race relationships in South Africa, cry to be made a garden of Christ. And how shall Christ answer our prayer unless we become his clergy and missionaries, with his own gallant and sacrificing spirit. It is not a change in government we require, but a change in men. We want clean shirts. Renew a right spirit within me.

So in the faith that neither life nor death can separate us from the love of God in Christ Jesus our Lord, I summon you to love in the light of your everlasting destiny, knowing that if we suffer with Christ, we shall also reign with him. The old pagan warriors cried to home-staying citizens as they left for battle: "We who are about to die, salute you." But the warriors of Christ exclaim: "We who are about to live, salute you."

(A different version of this sermon is called: "Resurrection of Christendom.")

PART THREE

Preaching in a World in Crisis
(America)

21

Communion Devotion: The Realism of the Gospel

The minister understands that the Church is a shelter for the weary, but that it also has to shake complacency. The actions and parables of Christ exemplify the educational realism of the Gospel: the Prodigal Son, tired of living in sties; Judas ashamed of his concupiscence; parishioners, tired of cliques, etc . . . Jesus anticipates the Cross, cures the possessed, washes dirty feet and forgives the sneers and cruelty of both the ignorant and the chosen people. With no time for indifference, Christianity needs a visionary program.

JOHN KEATS, THE DREAMING poet, once wrote: "I will clamber through the clouds and exist. I will get such an accumulation of stupendous recollections that as I walk through the suburbs of London I may not see them." There goes a man who shut his eyes to reality.

I once met a man, an auctioneer who had a voice like a roaring-bulldog and was always asking me to face up to facts. When he died, his house and the contents fell under the auctioneer's hammer. The sale-rooms were crowded and I took a walk in the garden, until the sale should begin. There I noticed a well-built concrete shelter. And on the white-wash of it, there was a circle of wood. On that was painted a white dove. Under it was the inscription: "Peace-haven." The world was at war, but he was most certainly at peace. That was not a man; that was an ostrich.

Some people, I fear, come to Church as a funk-hole: an air-raid shelter, where the hard realities of the world are forgotten by a temporary flight into Cloud-Cuckoo Land. God knows people need spiritual comfort these days; and those who rely on the mighty promises of God gain help for life's welfare. But they come to Church not to forget the world, but that they may see it in the right perspective.

I am certain that it is the duty of the Church to encourage, but also to exhort; to soothe the over-worried, but also to pin-prick the conscience; to comfort the sad, but to dislodge the complacent. For that reason I take as my theme the realism of the Gospel. The Gospel is not always a warm bath; it is often a cold shower. It is sometimes chloroform, but it is also a tonic.

I have spoken to you before how our magnificent faith enables us to meet the three fiercest foes of human life: sin, suffering and death. I want to show this morning how it enables us to face life, and more, to transform it.

The vocabulary of the New Testament gives little opportunities of escapism. Listen to these words: nothing shadowy, uncertain or indefinite about them. "I will send the spirit of truth . . . Ye shall receive power . . . My meat is the will of my Father . . . I am the light of the world, the bread of life and the water of life . . . I am come that they might have life." These words have a quality of thickness about them.

Life is depicted in the Bible is hard; and to face up to God is part of its hardest. Saul the king, summing up his life found that you remember he said: "I have played the fool."

David felt the lash when he heard the prophet's words: "Thou art the man."

Pilate who lost the unruffled calm of Civil Servant, was embarrassed and uncomfortable in the presence of the King of Kings.

Supremely is our Lord's life one of realism: "The three central points of that life are summed up by three symbols: a cradle, a gallows, and a tomb (if an empty one). It began with a child's cry and his earthly life ceased with a sigh."

How Christ knew our human nature: he had no illusion about it. Here is no rose-water view of life; no chirping Browning like an impertinent sparrow saying "God's in His Heaven, all's right with the world.". But what comes out is the agonized soul's cry of dereliction: "My God, my God, why hast thou forsaken me?"

He anticipated the Cross long time before he came to it. He knew that human nature, despite its pretty promises of discipleship, could in a wild burst of passion, pin the Holy One of God to a tree. He knew that when it acted thus, it was in ignorance. "Father, forgive them for they know not what they do."

He knew that human nature was capable of running away from God to a far country and filthying itself in a sty. But he knew that when it had become dissatisfied with the piggeries, it would return longing for the cleanliness of God.

He knew that Judas was capable of selling the ideal in a dirty bargain for thirty pieces of silver. He knew also, that when he realized the bargain he had made, he would go away and hang himself in the dark on a tree.

You who purr about the earthly beauty of Christ; you who cuddle up to the comfort of God, realize the Savior of life came not to bring peace but the sword. He leaped over the fences that divide men into their coteries and clubs and cliques. This Gospel that he was and preached was a "vulgar" gospel. Vulgar, in its original sense, meant for the crowd. I quote the words of the late A. E. Whitham: "It is not elegant. If it had grace, it is the grace of washing dirty feet of travel-stained men; the grace of wrestling with slobbering-mouthed lunatics and devil-possessed creatures; the grace of a tortured body on hard bits of timber, with a jeering crowd, amid gambling soldiers and an undertone of grief-stricken mothers and penitent prostitutes with the stench of death and the loamy whiff of the grave."

The Cross of the Incarnate Son of God is not an ecclesiastical ornament; an attractive badge for button-hole. It is the very height and depth of God's realism. It is the wound of God set close to the wound of the world. The reality of costly redemption meets the reality of desperate human need, telling us the ugly awkward truth about ourselves and offering us the conquest.

By altering one line of Studert-Kennedy's poem, I stress the urgency of a return to the Savior of the world; the need of a living Church which would not betray:

> When Jesus came to Wallington, they simply passed him by;
> They never hurt a hair of Him; they only let Him die;
> For men had grown more tender, and they wouldn't give Him pain
> They only just passed down the street and left Him in the rain.

It is this indifference to him, this patronizing attendance at his worship, this unwillingness to commit one's self to the fullest Church cooperation, this Christianity with reserves, which is to crucify him afresh in the eyes of the world. I plead with you as we are about to meditate on his sufferings for the world; and to receive the benefits of his sacrifice. I plead with you: Do you want to see him passed by, overlooked by the world? Or do you want to see him come into his royal rights as the Lord of all Life?

Then Christianity must be a program, not a hobby, a sheer necessity, not a luxury. And that responsibility rests on you, not on the Prime Minister, the Mayor, the Clergy, but on you.

22

Dangerous Silence

The saying that "speech is silver and silence is gold" is reconsidered here. There are two kinds of silence: one is the silence of wonder and patience; the other, the silence of contempt or cowardice, exemplified in the denial of Peter. Taking the example of the four lepers, this peroration is an encouragement to witness to Christ and to evangelize the nations.

- 2 Kings 7:9: "We do not well: this is a day of good tidings, and we hold our peace: now therefore come that we may go and let us tell the king's household."

THERE ARE MANY KINDS of silence that the Bible illustrates. There is the deep silence of *reverence*: the silence that is induced by thinking of the wonderful and mysterious ways of God. We are told that Abraham sent his faithful servant to look out for a wife for his son Jacob. The servant prayed to God that as he stood at the well of the city of Nahor, the first maiden who should offer him water for himself and his camels should be Isaac's bride-to-be. Rebecca came to the well. Then, says the Holy Writ: "And the man looked steadfastly on her, holding his peace." He *marveled* in silence how God had kept his promise.

The centuries pass by. There is a council meeting of the early Church in Jerusalem. Men rebuke Peter for daring to eat with the Gentiles, mere outsiders. He tells them of his vision in which God rebukes him for daring to call unclean anything that God has made. He concludes: "What was I, that I could withstand God? When they heard these things, they held their peace." Again, here is the silence of reverence, for God has graciously seen fit to include the Gentiles in the plan of salvation.

Then there is another kind of peace: the peace or silence of *patience*. Isaiah rebukes the Jews for their rebelliousness, idolatry, and lasciviousness. He ends the harangue with a plea to remember the patience of God: "Have I not held my peace even of a long time and thou fearest me not." This is an amazing silence. Man flaunts God, derides and insults him, yet God refuses to take revenge. He waits; his patience is inexhaustible.

Then, again, there is another peace, a silence more eloquent than words—the silence of *contempt*. Jesus stands before Caiaphas, the High Priest, to be tried for his life. The trial is a mockery of justice. The accusations made against our Lord are put forward by paid false witnesses. The High Priest turns to Jesus: "Answerest thou nothing? What is it which these witnesses hold against thee?" But Jesus held his peace. O eloquent silence!

All these silences mentioned so far, are *wise* silences—the result of forethought and discipline. But there is a silence that is *dangerous*. That is the theme of this story from the Second Book of Kings.

Samaria, the capital of Judah, was in a state of siege. The enemy, King Ben-Hadad of Syria, was at the gates. His aim was to starve the citizens of Samaria into surrender. Food prices had risen to fantastic heights. The head of an ass was sold for ten pounds of silver and dove's dung realized twelve shillings a pint. In fact the situation was so desperate that mothers were driven to boiling their own children for food.

Outside the city gates were four lepers. Their situation too was desperate. If they stayed where they were, they would die. If they entered the famine-stricken city, they would die of starvation. Their only forlorn hope was to go over to the camp of the besieging army. The Syrian soldiers might kill them, or they might give them food. To stay meant a lingering death; to go meant the possibility of a quick death, or even perhaps food. They set off for the Syrian camp in the twilight.

To their amazement, when they reached the outlying tents, they found them deserted. Not a man was in sight. The inhabitants had obviously decamped in a desperate hurry, for they had left all their possessions behind them. In the first tent they entered the lepers ate and drank their fill. They found plates and goblets of gold and silver, and rich silks and satins. They carried them away and went to another tent in search of loot. Here again they found the same rich food, ornaments and clothes, and they hid these, hoping, perhaps, to dig them up later.

You can imagine the joy of these lepers. They were the outcasts of society. Their loathsome disease prevented them from living a normal life in community. They were tramps who depended on the generosity of wild nature, or the scraps that the healthy would throw to them. They eked out a hand-to-mouth existence from day to day. Then, unexpectedly, when they were prepared for sudden death, they became richer than their wildest dreams. There was a feast fit for kings, and they gulped it greedily; there were riches which they might exchange for food, for years to come. Their happiness was complete. Now they could be revenged on the society that had rejected them and left them to die, or merely gave an edge to their starving appetites by throwing them scraps. Let the citizens of Samaria perish in their famine! Now the tables are turned! But even while they ate, there were specters at the feast. They could not forget the city where doves' dung was a delicacy, and where mothers had to boil their own babies for food.

Then they said one to another: "We do not well. This is a day of good tidings, and we hold our peace: if we tarry till the morning light, punishment will overtake us. No, therefore come, let us go and tell the king's household." So off they went, to tell the starving city that there was bread for their empty stomachs. They raced to the king to tell him that his foe Ben-Hadad had been routed. How right they were! It was a day of good-tidings and it would have been criminally selfish to hold their peace.

Isn't this a word of God to us today? "This is a day of good-tidings. And we hold our peace." The everlasting Gospel of the blessed God has to be proclaimed. A failure to witness is criminal in two ways:

1. It is disloyalty to Christ. His last command was: "Go ye therefore and make disciples of all nations." Do you remember the day when Peter found out his disloyalty and wept bitterly because he had not spoken a word for Christ? His Lord was being tried for his life and Peter was warming his hands at the fire of the outer courtyard. Suddenly, a maid caught a glimpse of his rugged fisherman's profile in the darting firelight, and instantly recognized him. "Ah," she said, "You were with the Nazarene too, with Jesus!"

That was Peter's chance to witness, to protest his Master's innocence, to declare his power, to proclaim his teaching. But he failed Christ there. So is every Christian who will not proclaim the Lordship of Christ over his life. If Jesus is the King of Kings, is there anything to be ashamed of in being his herald? If Christ has transformed your life, transfigured your outlook, given you inner peace, a new love for your fellow-men and a radiant confidence that sin, and suffering, and death are conquered by his power, then advertise it. For this is the living proof of your loyalty. "He that is not with me is against me," said Jesus.

The company of Christ's friends exists, not as a closed corporation of shareholders driving preference dividends; it exists to promote the unlimited sway of Christ over the whole world that is his. We worship that we may witness. We are silent before God so that we may speak what he delivers to us, to all people. "We do not well. This is a day of good tidings and we hold our peace." Do you want to estimate your worth as a disciple? Here is an infallible test. How many men and women have been inspired by your loyalty to Christ to join his Church? If you have not won a single soul for our Lord, then you do not well to hold your peace. Obviously the love of Christ is not streaming through your life to your fellows. You are a dirty window obscuring his holy light; you are a rusty door, through which Christ cannot find entry to his own. But if one single soul has known the ineffable peace and joy of the Christian life, then you are a true disciple, and Christ acknowledges you.

2. Silence concerning Christ is criminally selfish, too. The lepers had no right to keep food from the starving citizens of Samaria. Christians have no right to deprive the spiritually starving citizens of the world of the Bread of Life. Do you know how John Bunyan was won for Christ? By the excited talk of four women, who could not contain themselves as they spoke of the difference Christ had made to their lives. There he stood, the tinker of Bedford, with pots and pans in one hand and tools in the other, listening spellbound to four simple women, as they sat in the sun. They were so full of the regenerating power of Christ that they could not keep it in. And one loving heart set another on fire: "This is a day of good tidings and we cannot hold our peace."

Let us suppose, as we should, that you are convinced that Christ is the way, the truth, and the life, and that the evils of old are due to the lack of Gospel, then, what can you do to witness?

Two things:

1. Support your Church. Do you think our meetings here at 11:00 a.m. and at 6:30 p.m. are simply for our own good? Not they. They are a sermon to the world in themselves. They tell the outside world: "Here is a company of men and women who rule their lives by the standards and the power of Christ. We stand as a witness to the centrality of Christ." This is witness. But if your churchgoing is casual, occasional, and rare, how can

your friends and neighbors believe that you are seriously, desperately in earnest about the cause of Christ? As surely as on these dark evenings the light streams through glazed windows in our churches to the darkness outside, we stand for the light of the Gospel of God that shines in the face of Jesus Christ, the Light of the world.

2. You can do another thing. You and I may feel that our duty lies in this country. Home ties keep us here. We cannot go abroad as missionaries of the Gospel. But we can send missionaries out in Christ's name. It is our purses and prayers that do that. And that is witness!

If we did only these two things with absolute sincerity, then we should be proving our loyalty to Christ, and our devotion to our fellowmen. We could never say of ourselves: "We do not well. This is a day of good-tidings and we hold our peace." We should bear branded on our souls the marks of the Lord Jesus.

23

The Threat of Secularism

Sermon Preached in America

This sermon was written in the sixties in America where, because of geographic and social mobility, the Church serves, additionally, as a community gathering center. Yet, as the Body of Christ, it sometimes fails to face the larger problems of socio-economic and interracial integration, and of feeding the soul. Here is an appeal for the Church's return to the Imitatio Christi, *with his balanced blend of worldly duties and otherworldly concerns.*

BEFORE WE GO ANY further, let's define our terms. What is secularism? In the Oxford dictionary there are two meanings applicable to religion. The first is *worldly*: it would clearly be a threat to the life of the Christian Church if it were worldly, and tried to compete for the attention of the people with worldly inducements. This I shall consider later in greater detail. The second meaning in the dictionary is *skeptical of religious truth*. Here again, a Church of non-believers would be a contradiction of terms; and [would] such a Church with a message, without conviction, have the right to exist? The question then is this: is the Church today threatened most dangerously from within by worldliness and skepticism?

In my judgment, it is. Some would say that we see not so much a Church threatened and challenged by secularism, as one collapsing from it. This has been judged the post-Christian age. Others have called it the age when God is dead. Yet others have claimed that the man of today has a hole in his head, and it is a God-shaped vacuum.

Where, then, are we to mark the cracks in the walls of the temple of God?

1. One suggestion is that secularism, worldliness, is to be seen in our confused understanding of the purpose of the Church of Christ. Will

Herberg of Drew University has suggested that for the modern American, the Church is merely a symbol of togetherness. America, as we know, is a country of great mobility; every year, one family in every five moves its home. America is also the melting pot of nations. Its problem is to create community rapidly. This is the justification that many give for the churches. But we must note that the churches reflect the class, social, and cultural divisions of the world. There are Negro churches and White churches; there are elegant Episcopal or Presbyterian churches for the affluent, and there are Pentecostal storefront churches for the artisans. Vance Packard, in *The Status Seekers*, has shown that different denominations carry status symbols.

Now I contrast this togetherness, this social conformity according to my preferred group, with the life of the Early Church, where Jew and Greek, Roman aristocrat and Syrian slave, knelt together, to receive the Holy Communion; and I am bound to say that this was a world-denying Church, and ours is a world-affirming Church. I don't think our sin is pride; it is complacency, smug satisfaction with being in the in-group and letting the out-groups take care of themselves. We are dying of inbred respectability.

How else do we conceive the purpose of a Church? As a mutual protection-society, I suggest. Not to be sure as a fire-insurance society against the flames of Hell; we are too modern for that. But most certainly we consider the Church as a mutual protection society against the winds of change, and the uncomfortable realities of the world outside.

How often have I heard of the Church defended against attacks, as a good place for young people, because, if they have their dances on the Church premises, they won't be tempted to pet in cars or go to low dives? How often have I heard a minister's sermons praised because they are so very comforting? The implication of this is plainly that in a world of rapid social and intellectual change in which the three major bombs of Darwin, Marx, and Freud have rocked us to our foundations, and revolution and adaptation are the order of the day, Christians hope, like inelegant ostriches, to face the world with their backsides to the wind and their heads firmly embedded in the warm, soothing sands. That is why there is such a demand for cults like Christian Science, which claims there is no evil, no sin, no death, no suffering; that is why positive thinking supporters find Norman Vincent Peale so appealing and St. Paul so appalling!

How does this square with the challenge of the Christ who told his Jewish followers that a despised Samaritan was a better man than their own official exponents of religion, the priests of the Levites? Where is the challenge of him who summoned his adherents to "take up the gallows, bear their cross," and follow him? How does this square with a faith that, when it celebrates the Holy Communion, takes broken bread and poured-out wine as symbols of his body torn on the Cross and his blood that oozed out for the redemption of the world?

2. If there is appalling worldliness in the Church in its social conformity and its failure to face the intellectual and practical problems of today with Christian faith and confidence, there is also skepticism in its thinking.

We shall never recover the authority of the Christian Church as God's people with a message and a life grounded upon the divine will, unless our thinking and our acting returns to the source: Divine Revelation in the Holy Scriptures. I am not pleading for Fundamentalism—I understand the "fun" of it, and the "damn" in it, but I cannot always discover the "mental"—but I am pleading for a return to the central conviction that, in Christ, we have fully demonstrated the love and purpose of God, and in his life, the supreme example of how people should live, and in his Church, the possibility of the Beloved Community overcoming the alienations, divisions, and snobberies of the world.

Let us argue less about his relevance, and strive more to submit ourselves to his holy and cheering will. I am frankly tired of the attempts to dilute his truth, to compromise his stern demands, to be expedient and cautious, instead of daringly confident and adventurous in faith. I think he offers a daringly realistic faith. In the Gospel, we see that, because of the Crucifixion, we cannot accept a superficial pessimism. "In this world ye shall have tribulations. But be of good cheer, I have overcome the world." I admire in him the perfect balance between this-worldly duty and other-worldly hope that the Church must recover.

3. I could also speak of the financial evaluation of the ministry and of the Church in Old South Church, Boston. But this will be for another time.

A comparison: I would like to compare a devastating satire on the worldly Church with what I believe is a truer account of its real purpose. The satire comes from Peter de Vries's novel, *The Mackerel Plaza*. The minister of the People's Liberal Church, in suburban plush Connecticut, is convinced that Jesus was only a first century Oscar Wilde, and that he can improve on the Sermon of the Mount. This Hemingway of the pulpit, with his slick, streamlined ten-minute-sermons, believes the major problem is to stop his young people from killing themselves off in hot-rods or sports cars. He therefore produces an improved slogan for road hogs that improves on the Sermon on the Mount: "Blessed are the pacemakers, for they shall see God." His culture-accommodating gospel and church are finely exposed in the tour he takes of the "plant."

> OUR Church is, I believe, the first split-level church in America. It has five rooms and two baths downstairs, dining area, kitchen and three parlors for committee and group meetings, with a crawl space behind the furnace ending in the hillside into which the structure is built. Upstairs is one huge all-purpose interior, divisible into different-sized compartments by means of sliding walls and convertible into an auditorium for putting on plays, a gymnasium for athletics and a ballroom for dances.

The emphasis on social facilities as the be-all and end-all of the Church is typical of a church where secularism has prevailed. There's yet to mention specifically religious activities. But here it comes:

> There is a small worship area at one end. This has a platform cantilevered on both sides, with a freeform pulpit designed by Noguchi. It consists of a slab of marble set on four legs of delicately differing fruitwoods, to symbolize the four gospels and their failure to harmonize. Behind it dangles a large multicolored mobile, its interdenominational parts swaying, as one might fancy, in perpetual reminder of St. Paul's criticism against "those blown about by every wind of doctrine . . ." In the back of this building is a newly erected clinic with medical and neuro-psychiatric wings, both indefinitely expandable. Thus the People's Liberal Church is a church designed to meet the needs of today, and to serve the whole man. This includes the worship of a God free of outmoded theological definitions and palatable to a mind come of age in the era of relativity.

Notice there the three signs of a Church utterly overwhelmed by secularism: 1. its subordinate conformism; 2. its insistence upon comfortable security and good health; 3. the skepticism that frees itself from the embarrassment of the Gospel.

Contrast this with the image that Dick Sheppard had of the church called the parish church of the British Commonwealth, St. Martin-in-the Fields, in Trafalgar Square, in the heart of London:

> I stood on the west steps and saw what this church would be to the life of the people. They past me, into its warm inside, hundreds and hundreds of all sorts of people, going up to the temple of their Lord, with all their difficulties, trials and sorrows. I saw it full of people, dropping in at all hours of the day and night. It was never dark, it was lighted all night and all day, and often and often tired bits of humanity swept in.

We have had the Social Gospel; we need it again. We have never had in its fullness the interracial Gospel; we need it desperately, as do the victims of prejudice, and the prejudiced whose brains need to be "Christ-washed" and made color-blind.

THREE FUNCTIONS OF THE TRUE CHURCH

Surely the function of Christ's Church is:

1. To proclaim in its preaching and to renew in its worship the universal Gospel of the grace of God, which stoops to conquer in the Incarnation of Jesus Christ, his ministering life, sacrificial death, and hope-creating Resurrection. That is its chief function, outgoing in its witness.

2. Secondly, its purpose is to be the arena of the radically mind-and-heart-changing power of the Holy Spirit (Story of red shirts, brown shirts, and clean shirts ...)

3. Thirdly, such a community consecrated to God and dedicated to man, needs to be the living embodiment of the new humanity in which the world's status symbols are left, where they ought to be left, on the mat outside the Church, in the dirt where they belong. This is the cure for secularism, for the Church to be the Church that Christ loved and gave himself for.

Then the Church will be confident in faith, radiant in hope, and all-welcoming in its charity.

24

The Gospel and the Reversal of Human Values

Here is a presentation of the Social Gospel and of Jesus the Reformer, in direct succession to Moses, who brought back the Law to the worshippers of Mammon. The parable of the rich man who, living for security, gets his rewards on earth and hell in the after-life, and of Lazarus, whose journey is exactly the opposite, teaches not to be deceived by so-called "success." Through a quick survey of the Gospel, the story is linked to the messages given in the Sermon on the Mount, Paul's Letter to the Romans, ch. 12, Jesus's affirmation of Peter, and the parable of the Great Supper. Christianity is reaffirmed as the religion of the poor and the afflicted. The Christian, living by faith and charity, is encouraged to live in humility and service for a classless society where all are servants of each other.

- Luke 14:12–14: "Then Jesus said to his host: 'When you give a luncheon or dinner, do not invite your friends, your brothers or relatives, or your rich neighbors; if you do, they may invite you back and so you will be repaid. But when you give a banquet, invite the poor, the crippled, the lame, the blind, and you will be blessed. Although they cannot repay you, you will be repaid at the resurrection of the righteous.'" (*New International Version*)

- Luke 16:13: "No servant can serve two masters. Either he will hate the one and love the other, or he will be devoted to the one and despise the other. You cannot serve both God and Money." (*New International Version*)

- Luke 16:19–31: (the parable of the rich man and Lazarus)

THE FIRST CHRISTIANS WERE radical revolutionaries. Where they were bold, we are fearful. Where they were willing to stand up and be counted, we slink into shadows. And so, the present day Church counts for very little. They were like the Gospel, the good news; we are old hat; stale, customary, conventional, so predictable. It was said of the first generation of Christians: these are they who have turned the world upside down. It could only be said of us: "The world has turned them downside up!"

Despite Christ's warning that we cannot serve God and Mammon, that is, God and the standards of this world, we seem satisfied with our diet of blood-red steak and an afterthought of angel-cake, with having a good time, making a good thing out of this world, and giving one hour to God and the good news once a week, or once a fortnight. We like to combine the Gospel and ten per cent profit, God and the American way of life. But God is not a good American, nor Jesus Christ a bright young man with Brooklyn associations who always urges the faithful to vote for the Democratic ticket. And Christians are not meant to be nice, harmless, safe, wouldn't hurt a fly kind of people.

Our Lord told two rather unusual stories to make it clear that Christianity or the Kingdom of God is the reversal of human values; that God's rule overturns all worldly estimates and values. As Jesus put it: "For that which is highly esteemed among men is abomination in the sight of God" (Luke 16:15).

Side by side in the same village, there lived two men. One was unnamed, because though he might look important, [he] was unimportant and not worth remembering. He lived like a lord, splendidly clothed in white linen and purple silk, and his menus matched his millinery. He fared sumptuously every day. The other man, Lazarus, was to be seen each day at the rich man's gate, begging from the crumbs that fell from the rich man's table. Not a very attractive looking man, for it is recorded that the dogs licked his sores.

The thumbnail sketch has already made it clear who was the success in life and who was the failure. The rich man had money, position, power, health, and so, success. The poor man had nothing but poverty and sickness. I can imagine the rich man saying to his servants: "Don't give Lazarus too many crumbs, that lazy good-for-nothing, or he'll come to depend on my bounty. Let him get up and go out and earn his living, the dirty bum. Where is his self-respect?" Yet it is the rich man who goes to Hell: he has loved only himself, and he can hug himself forever in eternity, as his due. It is the poor man who goes to heaven. Isn't that the complete reversal of human values?

Yet there is one very attractive feature in the rich man: even though he knows he has forfeited eternal life, he is anxious that his five brothers shall escape his destiny. Landed in Hell, he cries out to Father Abraham, asking him to send Lazarus to dip his finger in water and cool the heat of the rich man's tongue in the discomfort of Hell. Abraham replies: "Son, remember that you in your lifetime received the good things, and Lazarus the bad things; but now he is comforted and you are troubled." Then the rich man asked Abraham to send Lazarus as a messenger to the five brothers of the rich man to warn them, lest they suffer the same fate. But Abraham sternly replied: "Your brothers have the five books of Moses and the writings of the prophets; let them be warned by them!" "But," said the rich man, "the warning would be much more effective if it was carried to them by a man who has returned from the dead." Inexorable, Abraham replies: "If they won't pay heed to Moses and the prophets, they won't listen even to a resurrected man."

Now if this were a series of sermons and not just a single one, we could think of the many contrasts between a Christian man and the worldly man, such as those depicted in the Sermon on the Mount or Paul's Letter to the Romans, chapter 12. A man of the world lives by insurances, whereas a Christian does not worry about to-morrow. Sufficient unto the day is the evil thereof. A man of the world hits back when he is hit; a Christian turns the other cheek. A man of the world harbors resentment; a Christian forgives seven times seventy times. A man of the world gathers treasures and status symbols on earth; a Christian man lays up treasures in heaven where moth and rust cannot destroy his good trust. All this is true. And so different were the Christians from those around them in the first century that St. Paul said they were "not many wise, not many noble," but mere nobodies, all the better to show the power of God in their lives.

In this parable of Jesus, which I have been retelling, there are two great contrasts between the Christian and the world, and it is these I want us to concentrate on.

Notice first that the despised of the world are exalted in Christ's Kingdom. Christ did not say: "On this Rockefeller I will build my Church," but on this Rock, meaning on those who, like Peter, confessed his Messiahship, and saw Jesus as the Lord of History and of their lives. Jesus told another story of two sets of invitations to the Great Supper of his Kingdom. Those to be invited first sent back excuses of refusal: one wanted to measure or fertilize some land he had just bought; another had bought five yoke of oxen, and wanted to try them out; another was newly married, and not much interested in outside events. Though invited, they loved the world first. So a second set of invitations had to be sent. The host sent his servant into the byways, to bring in the poor, the maimed, the halt, and the blind. Surely this means that the smugly complacent have no place in the Kingdom of God; it is the imperfect and the unhappy, those conscious of failure and of handicap in life, who respond to the call of Christ and his Kingdom.

The Gospel offers comfort to all of you, for whom life has been a hard and bitter struggle against temptation, poverty, and all handicaps: "Blessed are the poor in spirit for theirs is the kingdom of heaven." And to you for whom life has been comfortable—one uninterrupted success story—the Gospel is a warning: "It is harder for a camel to go through the eye of the needle than for a rich man to enter the Kingdom of God." The warning is that you cannot take it with you; that you be not possessed by your possessions, but by the scale of values set up by God, for whom love of him and love of neighbor come first and last.

The second thing this parable teaches us is that the Christian lives not by the cold eye of reason, but by the bright eye of faith. By it Jesus says to us: "Don't be fooled by the brittle promises of this world that break as easily as pie-crusts or melt as rapidly as ice-cream in ninety-degree-weather. The world is visible, all too visible, so that we are blinded by its dazzle and roar, forgetting that God made visible things, that they might point us to the invisible. If God made the rose so beautiful, what must we be like?"

Man shall not live by bread alone, but by every promise that proceedeth out of the Word of God. We all live by promises: the child by the promise of Christmas; the husband and wife by the promises and vows of fidelity they made on their marriage day; businessmen by the promise implicit in every check to pay the bearer; and we Christians live by the sterling promises of God, sealed and signed in his Son, Jesus Christ.

To live by faith is to live as those who trust the promises of God in Christ: "In this world ye shall have tribulation; but be of good cheer, for I have overcome the world." "In my Father's house are many mansions: I go to prepare a place and where I am you shall be also. If it be not so, I would have told you." "Lo, I am with you always even unto the end of the world."

As Luther said, the promises of God are the wedding rings by which he attaches us to himself forever and ever.

Notice that in this parable, Jesus does not argue us into accepting the reality of the two alternative destinations for the human soul. He does much more: he assumes it. This is how things are in God's eternal Kingdom: "Believe and rejoice, for God is faithful."

Thirdly and lastly, we see the reversal of human values in the life of Jesus Christ himself. The world's way is to get rich; the Christ's way is to become poor for our sake. I shall never cease to be humbled by the greatness of Christ's miracles and by the Incarnation, when the eternal Son of God and prince of Heaven, became the servant of all though he was Lord of all. We marvel at Abraham Lincoln's ascent from log cabin to the White House; we should marvel even more at our Lord's descent from the whitest of Houses to an outhouse of an inn, to despised and rejected in Bethlehem, and of whom it was said: "Foxes have holes and the birds of the air have nests, but the Son of Man hath nowhere to lay his head," and for whom a borrowed grave had to be found for three days, before he tore the rock, and rose again. Here the young prince got out and walked.

May God give you the inner eye of faith to discern that all men are neighbors; that the Kingdom is the true classless society and an everlasting Kingdom; and that humility and service are its signs, and God alone its supreme Governor!

25

A Victorious Faith Conquering Prejudice

*The Church as a Local Community
Preached at Brookfield Congregational Church,
Connecticut, July 19, 1959*

Community life in the Church means victory over cynicism, pride and conventions and opening up to friendship and love. Courage is exemplified by two women, mistress and servant, who shared the same martyrdom, as equals. After a satirical portrait of the Church as country-club, drawn from Peter de Vries, the virtues of the Christian are stated: forgiveness over vindictiveness; faith and trust over skepticism; integration over racism; and neighborliness over affectation.

> Acts 2:44–47: "And all who believed were together and had all things in common: sold their possessions and goods, and parted them to all, as they had need. And day by day, continuing steadfastly with one accord in the temple, and breaking bread at home, they took their food with gladness and singleness of heart, praising God, and having favor with all the people. And the Lord added to them day by day those that were saved." (*American Standard Version*)

OUTSIDE THE NEW-BORN CHURCH there was terrible alienation: man against man, and man cursing the God who made him with every disappointment. Inside the Church reigned a remarkable community-life, all deriving from the victory of Christ, in Cross and Resurrection, over the cynicism and materialism of the world, over the pride and prejudices that split men into antagonistic groups, and over the fear of conventionalities that prevent men going forward in faith. Outside the Church there was isolation and alienation, and anxiety; inside the Church one found faith in God through Christ, and a friendship that shared everything.

The first Church of Christ was a Community Church, and its story to the outsiders was: "Look, God has overcome our differences and suspicions. This is the work of the Holy Spirit. Come and join us." And the surprised Jews and Greeks said, not in sarcasm, but in sober testimony: "How these Christians love one another!"

The years passed and the small minority movement of Christians would not bow the knee to a Caesar who claimed to be God. So Caesar determined to crush their protests in the dust, in the arena. There had been men martyrs before, like old Bishop Polycarp in his eighties, who was willing to be crushed by the teeth of the lions, that God might sift the good from the evil in him. But I now speak of a marvel: two women martyrs, witnesses to the crucifixion and resurrection of Christ—the weaker sex, physically frail, but made almost fearless by faith. The two women who cling together in the Coliseum of Rome and wait for the order for the lions to be loosed from their pits are Felicitas and Perpetua, a Roman aristocrat matron and her servant maid, with the bonds of snobbery and class-consciousness annihilated in faith.

How different is the world! It is all very well for the sentimental to say: "The Colonel's lady and Judy O'Grady are sisters under the skin. But look at the difference of the skins and what's on them: the Colonel's lady uses Lanvin and Judy O'Grady essence of wallflowers or lily of the valley; the Colonel's lady wears the skunk's wealthiest cousin, mink; and Judy has imitation leopard-skin; and all the accessories, and husbands and cars, and houses to match." And this is how pride and envy are built up, so that two folk made in the image of God are ready to snarl when they meet. In the early Church, or in some churches today where the love of Christ and a sense of common need unite, the Colonel's lady and Judy O'Grady would be sharing their diversified experience of life, each learning how the other half lived, and each living for Christ and Christ's needy. Now it is much more likely that the Colonel's lady will be living in Westchester or Putnam Counties, and Judy in the Bronx. Or, if they lived both in Manhattan and, as good Irish Americans, they attended St. Patrick's Cathedral, they would worship in the same Church, but not at the same time: 7:00 a.m. Mass for Judy and the 11:00 a.m. High Mass [for the Colonel's lady], with all the choral accompaniments, Gregorian chanting, a sight of his Eminence Cardinal Spellman and the handsome Bishop Fulton Sheen televising his way into the affections, like God's ferret hunting for the female soul beneath the mink, or the male personality hiding behind the Brooks Brothers suit.

Now it was because many Christians, clerical and lay, believed that snobbishness and sanctity have nothing in common, and that Christ and caste are implacable foes, that they decided in our day to make a new type of Church: the Community Church. And, since Brookfield from all plans for future development is likely to expand in size and also to develop greater variety of families and income, thank God, I want to speak about the two possibilities that lie before it in the next fifteen years: to become an exclusive snob-shop, or a cell of the universal Body of Christ, a community of God open to experiment, and inclusive.

To help us visualize the possibilities, two American novelists of our time have depicted the closed and the open community church. Peter de Vries, that earthy rascal who lives in Connecticut, has provided in *The Mackerel Plaza* a witty warning of what a snob-shop for cultured intellectuals would be like at the People's Liberal Church in *Mackerel Plaza*. His description of the smack up-to-date church plant is a symbol of the supplying of modern man with what he says he wants, which is very different from what he needs. What he needs is to rediscover his unity with God and with the whole family of God. What the Church provides is psychiatry, preaching that is slick and short and shows off the minister instead of demonstrating Christ in his Gospel, and a guarantee that only nice country-club types with pale white faces or sallow sodden ones shall join. God cannot transform the Church because God is an outworn idea in the smart-alecky book; and neighbors with a sense of the tragic depths of life and the grace that comes to transform tragedy are excluded, or expected to be silent on such matters. This is the Church that has everything, the first split-level church in America. It has an indefinitely expandable sanitarium; rooms that can be used for dramatic performances; nurseries for children; conference centers; and as the spotty fish of a minister, Mr. Mackerel, takes us on the guided tour, he doesn't seem to notice that the sanctuary is the smallest part of the entire building, so impressed is he by its cultured appointments. After all, the free-standing pulpit has been designed by Noguchi, and it is supported by four delicately differing pillars of fruitwood to symbolize the contradictions between the four evangelists and, above it, [is] a mobile of hundreds of different pieces, which is moved by every breath, and [which] symbolizes the congregation blown by every wind of doctrine.

The minister is no better than the people. He approaches everything by turns, and nothing for long. He is flattered at being thought the Hemingway of the pulpit because his sermons are short and functional, and hard-boiled. He spends a week thinking out a slogan to cut down traffic accidents, one presumably that will improve on the Beatitudes: "Blessed are the pace-makers for they see God."

Jesus is for him neither the Son of God, nor the Son of man, neither crucified nor risen—only a first century Oscar Wilde—an iconoclast and a wit. Here is a tribal deity, made after the image of the culture mongers and snobs, who have measured out their lives with coffee-spoons. Self-made men, they worship their maker. Yes, this exclusive, modern and superbly aesthetic witty church has everything except God, except the crucified and risen Christ, except the transforming Holy Spirit, except the needy neighbor. It has everything, but it is nothing.

Then there is the open, inclusive, forgiving, healing type of community church in James Gould Cozzens's 1936 novel, entitled *Men and Brethren*. It happens to be an Episcopal Church in Manhattan; it could just as easily have been a Congregational Church in Connecticut. It has two ministers: the Vicar, Ernest Cudlipp, is certainly a man of sensitivity and culture, but not a snob. His door is always open at all hours and his plans are ever being interrupted by the clanging of the telephone. The Church presents the whole Gospel for the entire man, and for men in community. Radiating out from the central worship of the Church, its tribute of adoration to Christ, is a steady stream of social activities: social work, a medical clinic, and the cooperation of its members as a combined operation ministry to the depressed, to the would-be suicides, to the bored, to the bitter, hurt by life's cruelty.

The marks of this Church are seen in its two ministers: Cudlipp is intelligent compassion: the place of a servant of Christ is where need is, not congeniality. The mark of his assistant, Johnson, an old man who has given the best years of his life to the service of Alaska, is integrity of life and sacrifice. Cudlipp meditated when he looked into his elderly assistant's room and saw his only possessions: a picture of the barrenness and snow of Alaska and a group of converts in front of a simple shack of a church with a cross on it, a worn Bible and a copy of the *Imitation of Christ*. He thought that this old saint had all the infinite riches of Christ and the blessed joy of needing nothing more. The real test of a Community Church is not its plant, nor even that it is a historic church on the village green, it is simply its willingness to share all things in common—to be itself the parable of talents—open to the ways of God in the future.

What will its marks be?

1. It will overcome vindictiveness with forgiveness;
2. It will overcome skepticism with faith and trust;
3. It will overcome isolation from other races by being the inter-racial world-wide Church in its missionary concern and outreach;
4. And, it will overcome class snobbery by a genuine neighborliness.

And the source of all this flouting of conventions will be the God who broke the stereotype in Christ and, by his sheer generosity, welcomed the fifth columnist, Zacchaeus, the simple fisherman, Peter, the prostitute, Mary Magdalene, and the skeptic, Thomas—not because of their deserts, but because of their confessed need of him and love for him.

For individuals as for churches, God has appointed a way of life and a way of death. The way of death is the way of exclusiveness that says: "Thank God, I am not like other men;" and the way of inclusiveness and openness, which says: "If God can admit me to be a member of his Church, then no one need feel that Christ would turn him away."

"And all that believed were together and had all things in common." All things: yes, their possessions were voluntarily pooled, and they shared their worship, their attending the Lord's Supper, their benevolence to the orphans, the sick and those imprisoned for defying the Roman Emperor when he demanded to reign in the place that is alone Christ's, the young Prince of Life. And their lives had gratitude and joy; not drabness and misery. They had an open church; open to the call and challenge of God, heard in the ear, seen in the eyes, felt in the heart.

Let us pray [in the words of Hermann Hagedom]:

> Lord, in the hour of tumult,
> Lord, in the night of fears;
> Keep open, oh keep open,
> My eyes, my ears!
> Not blindly, not in hatred;
> Lord, let me do my part;
> Keep open, oh, keep open,
> My mind, my heart.

26

The World Church and Human Need

Delivered First at Mansfield College, Oxford

According to Davies's typical desire for ecumenicity, the World Church not only includes people of other faiths, but also atheists and agnostics still working in the vineyards of the Lord, who shake the conventional and shrunken Church from its complacency. The World Church includes all workers who serve humbly, in their professions, their trades and their callings—citizens who exercise their rights to work and vote.

THE NATURE OF THE WORLD CHURCH

THE CHURCH MILITANT ON earth numbers seven million persons, but the Church triumphant is literally—to human counting—numberless, for it consists of all those who, from the days of Abraham, lived by faith, not having received the promised Messiah, and those, who, since our Lord's coming in the flesh, of every race, of each sex, [and] of many different denominations, have put their trust in him, and proved it by their obedience:

> Seeing we are surrounded by so great a cloud of witnesses, let us run with patience the race that is set before us, looking to Jesus, the pioneer and perfector of our faith, who for the joy that was set before him endured the cross, despising the shame, and is now set down on the right hand of the throne of God.

It is in that wider context that the World Church on earth goes out to meet human need.

Because there is a World Church, and there are Christians in every land under heaven, clandestine in prohibited countries, open in countries where the proclamation of the Gospel is not prohibited or discouraged by the State, there is no longer any real division between "Foreign" and "Home" Missions. For every land is enemy occupied country and also every land is Holy Land, for Christ's servants also occupy it in his name. The only claim that one land has over another, for Christians, is its deeper need of the Gospel, of the grace of God, and of the spiritual and communal benefits the Gospel brings.

THE TASK OF THE WORLD CHURCH

If I had to sum it up in one sentence, I would say: "It is the task of the World Church to continue Christ's work of caring for the souls, bodies, and societies of men." When I say this, and confess gladly that this is the task of the Church of Christ, I do not want anyone to think that it is only acknowledged members of the Church of Christ who do this. God alone knows who belong to him; no pope, archbishop, or moderator can tell who the unacknowledged servants of Christ are, for God's merciful providence is mysterious, and those who seem to be fighting against the institutional Church may be of the number of God's servants.

It is possible that some agnostics, in their tirades against the complacency and flabbiness of the historic Church, do so in the interests of recalling the community of Christians to a simpler and deeper loyalty to the Christ of the early Church. We do well to remember that the heretics of one generation may become the saints of succeeding ones, that reformers and prophets of the living God may be denounced and denied for making the conventional uncomfortable. This was built for recalling the great Western Church to the uncorrupted simplicity of the Gospel. Luther was called a mad blasphemer, impudent dog by some of the leading ecclesiastics of his day, who clamored for his suppression. Michael Scott was described by an Archbishop of the Anglican Communion as "that restless, naive, neurotic fellow," and of the same man the President of a great educational foundation in New York said to me: "It was Michael Scott's stand at the U.N. on behalf of the Hirers that has helped me, as a Negro, to believe that Christ still has some white servants who are color-blind." "Christ loved the Church and gave himself for it that He might present it to himself without spot or wrinkle or blemish or any such thing."

The function of some of the greatest critics of the Church—and the atheists would qualify as such—is to remind us that there are spots, wrinkles, and blemishes that make the Church militant soft and complacent.

And, we must not forget the sincere adherents of other religions—Jews, Mohammedans, Hindus—also living up to the light which they have received, however dim or fitful, from their own religions; nor the many laymen who have dedicated themselves to the service of humanity, though they do not acknowledge the image of God in man. These are all outside the Church militant on earth, but many of them are fighting alongside it, in the battle against human want.

When this large allowance is made—that it is presumptuous for us to judge where God alone judges—that even agnostics and atheists have a critical function to perform in God's world and that, for the stimulation of God's Church, men of other faiths or humanists, also serve the God and Father of our Lord Jesus Christ, we must still assert that the Church is the instrument of the living God, the Body of which Christ is the Head, the saved and saving Community.

THE VARIETY OF ITS TASKS

The Second World Conference on Faith and Order defined the task of the Church as twofold: "Glorify GOD, adoration and sacrificial service." That means worship and service that is costly and costing witness. The Church faces God in the glad acknowledgement of how, in Christ, he has translated us from the kingdom of darkness into the kingdom of the love of his dear Son. The Church confesses her sins, receives the forgiveness of God, hears her marching orders in the Scriptures and preaching, remembers her fellowship in earth and heaven and her duties in the context of prayer, looks forward to her victory over sin, and suffering, and death, and joins with the crucified and risen Christ in the sacraments of Baptism and the Lord's Supper. In the same atmosphere the local Congregational fellowship meets under the inspiring and empowering influence of the Holy Spirit to fulfill her commitments in the life of the local community for Christ's sake.

It is only in the context of worship that we can receive the humility by which we can serve the world without patronage. This has been finely stated by the late Dr. Kenneth Kirk, formerly Bishop of Oxford:

> Yet apart from an atmosphere of worship, every act of service avails only to inflate the agent's sense of patronage. He is the doctor, humanity his patient: he is the Samaritan, his neighbor the crippled wayfarer: he is the instructor, others are merely his pupils.

> Gratitude (if they show gratitude) only confirms his conviction of his own importance; resentment (if they resent his services) only ministers to the glow of self-esteem with which he comforts himself in secret. (*Vision of God*. Abridged ed., 184)

Worship, by contrast, has as its centre a Cross, the dying-symbol of the life-giving son of God who became poor that we might become rich through him, who humbled himself, and calls for this mind in us. The primary task of the world Church is to give God his worth, his worship, and to let that recognition of God's worth send it out on errands of mercy. True worship of the living God is not a soporific, but a stimulus to service in humility.

THE TYPES OF SERVICE IN THE WORLD-CHURCH

Clearly there must be men and women trained in the art of *worship*, and of preaching, and administering the sacraments. There must be ministers and evangelists and pastors in the Church of God; for the ministry is a gift of Christ to his people for the leading of his flocks. They may minister in city or village churches; they may be chaplains in schools or hospitals, or factories; they may be teachers in theological colleges and universities, they may be administrators with secular calling for Christ's sake. And here we find a whole new range of activities which can be taken up to the glory of God.

In the underdeveloped countries in particular there is a demand for men and women to go out under government authority to undertake a multitude of tasks: engineers to construct bridges over ravines, or to build dams for water conservation, or channels for irrigation, and thus bring productivity where [there] was barrenness. Agriculturalists breed new hybrid crops or develop greater yields by the use of fertilizers or by teaching methods of soil conservation. Experts in forestry are needed to produce the timber for houses or fuel, or to assist in combating soil-erosion. Administrators are needed in the Colonial service to teach the art of self-government, so that they themselves will be no longer necessary when their pupils take over. Economists who will develop an industry or production engineers are needed. Geologists are required to prospect new sources of prosperity for underdeveloped regions and personalities. Sociologists are needed to make surveys of human problems in relation to environment; teachers of all the basic subjects are needed at junior and senior schools, and teachers' training colleges.

Hitherto these have been regarded as secular callings, but they are not; they are, if dedicated to God and the children of God, devout callings, sacred vocations. To this end the L. M. S. alone with several other Missionary Societies has developed a scheme of Association, so that those who go out to underdeveloped countries to fulfill such callings as may be linked with a local church, if there is one in their neighborhood, and keep them in touch with the homeland.

Their real importance is not the size of their responsibilities, but their faithfulness (as the parable of the talents shows). It is properly salutary for the publicized to remember, and consolatory for those who walk humbly with their God, that our Lord has declared that "the first shall be last and the last first." In this conference we do well to remember that there is no difference at all between the minister and the missionary—they are both sent by God to minister to his people, to build them up in the faith of Christ.

As one special example of what building a whole Church in worship and faith can mean, [one] would instance Alex Sandilands's preparation of a Book of Worship, including a confession of faith in the Tswana language for the Bechuanaland Christians in the Bechuanaland Protectorate to the North of Cape Province outside the Union of South Africa. The same task in our Congregational Churches in England is being undertaken by James Todd, Nathaniel and Romilly Micklem, John Huxtable and John Harsh, Kenneth Parry and Erik Routley, and—I might add—by every minister or layman who prepares for Sunday worship with understanding and care.

Social service for Christ's sake is undertaken by the doctors, nurses, medical orderlies and psychiatrists in many lands. It is done in the name of Christ to heal the souls and bodies of men. A notable example is Dr. Howard Somervell in India but not by any means the only example. Hurst tells of one visitor to Neyyoor who was impressed by the sight of a surgeon and nurses offering up a short prayer for Divine assistance over the patient who was about to be operated on. He comments: "Science in the hands of love."

Another category of worker in Christ's Church is the shaper of a Christian opinion, and that is the task of every Church member. This requires the courage that comes from faith in Christ and obedience to his dictates. I would illustrate it from the experience of a twenty-one year old missionary, Moffat, one who as to gifts was quite ordinary but became extraordinary under the inspiration of faith and obedience. The same is true of Livingstone.

Finally, let me close by reminding you that we are all missionaries—sent by Christ to care for his children—and that this may involve us in a multitude of varied duties, so that we become not specialists, but Jacks-of-all-trades: all things to all men, not because we are masters of none, but because our Master is one and he took a towel, and performed the menial tasks as an example. Here is what the most famous missionary of modern times wrote in his diary:

> Our house at the river Kolobeng . . . was the third which I had reared with my own hands. A native smith taught me to weld iron; and having improved by scraps of information in that line from Mr. Hoffat, and also in my carpentering and gardening, I was becoming handy at almost any trade, besides doctoring and aching; and as my wife could make candles, soap, and clothes, we came nearly up to what may be considered indispensable to the accomplishments of a missionary family in Central Africa, namely the husband to be a jack-of-all-trades without doors, and the wife a maid of all work within.

The modern missionary is likely to be a specialist, but he requires versatility and humility, as much as the pioneers, such as Dr. Alexander Kerr, first Principal at Fort Hare University College, in 1916.

This is a world without community, where men are herded by fear into opposing camps of suspicion: East and Western Germany split; European settlers and faithful Kikuyu on the one side, and the forest gangs of Key on the other; Bantu, Boer and Briton, at loggerheads in the Disunion of South Africa; suppressed minorities in Russia; Arab and Jew with guns cocked at the ready in Palestine; and the whole world wondering if the rapid end is to be part of a vast atomic crematorium.

The Christian soldier is one most needed, but he cannot be in all places at once and the needs are world-wide. How is he to become his brother's keeper? Partly by the World-wide Church (which I shall explain in the next lecture), but partly through exercising an intelligent interest in the ballot-box, and in returning men and women to Parliament "for whom the miseries of the world are miseries and who will not let them rest." Christ comes to the community partly through seven million Christians in the world, and partly through those who ignore or despise official Christianity because of its complacency and criticize the Church, but carry out Christ's work of caring, even under the defiant badge of atheism or agnosticism. But my one point is this: politics is the art through which I can love my far-off brothers; and our test for policies must be assistance to the needy, not as patronage, but as service and social justice as the consequence of the belief that men are made in the image of God and that Christ who died and rose again for them all.

27

Protests, Profound, and Trivial

A Baccalaureate Address Given at Lehigh University, June 11, 1967

∽ Acts 5:27–29 and Romans 12:2

FOR ALL OF US, graduands, parents, and friends ... trustees, administration and faculty, this is a time of gratitude and of questioning, of looking thankfully backwards and anxiously forwards.

As you look back over the past four years, it is something to be able to say: "I have survived." Some of you who have only just survived may feel as if you are about to be released from prison. But, in fact, a prison and a college are about as opposed as any two institutions could be; for it is easy to get into prison and hard to get out; whereas it is very hard to get into a good college and only too easy to flunk out. Never have the distracting influences exerted a stronger pull to drag you out of the cloister that is a college: the call to fight to desegregate our nation; the call to enlist in the Peace Corps or in the Marine Corps; and not least, the mating call. You graduands have suffered and survived everything from maleness to mononucleosis; from the breaking up of old prejudices and cherished convictions to learning that [those] who were a big fish in a small pool, are only a sardine in the world of scholarship. But you leave more mature.

Members of the faculty can also say they have survived the sometimes disillusioning experience of grading examinations and papers ... Yet everyone at Lehigh University naturally knows that Protestantism began when Martin Luther, professor of theology in the University of Wittenberg and an Augustinian monk, nailed a list of ninety-five brief topics for discussion on the door of the castle church, which he was ready to argue with the Papal envoy selling indulgences. The new slant that I received on the prodigious learning of Martin Luther was this: "The Reformation began in 1517 when Professor Luther nailed ninety-five Ph.D. theses on the door of the Castle Church in Wittenberg."

The other consolation in the degrading art of grading is the surprises that late developers and those who suddenly come alight from within spring upon their teachers. And I never fail to be delighted by those students who progress from being excited by spell-binders and super-anecdotalists, whom they think such fun in their freshman year, to an appreciation for those quieter teachers who have a deep dedication to high standards of scholarship and integrity, whom the student meets in his upper class years . . . So, the faculty, too, can say as they have watched your zigzag progression towards knowledge and mental, and moral maturity: "We too have survived."

It would be pleasant to continue in the vein of mutual congratulation, but I don't want to be a part of the bland leading the bland in these trying times. I have no sympathy at all with the bewildered clergy pictured in last week's *New Yorker* in the vestry after a service counting up the collection. The offertory plates are almost empty, and not only are there no dollar notes; there are only a few coins. It is clear that an uncomfortable sermon has been preached. The older clergyman turns to the younger and says: "Next week, back to the vague generalities."

I would rather address myself to the burning problem of the present—that of protests, profound and trivial. My two texts for this purpose are taken from The Acts of the Apostles, chapter 5, verses 27–29 and The Epistle to the Romans, chapter 12, verse 2. The first reminds us that the Christian Church was born when the disciples refused to be silent about the divine vindication of Jesus Christ through his resurrection with the shout: "We must obey God and not men." The second text is St. Paul's who has to remind the tiny Christian group in the capital of the greatest empire the world then knew that they must not, when in Rome, do as the Romans do, and sacrifice to the emperor as if he were divine. He says: "Be not conformed to this world, but be ye transformed by the renewing of your mind that you may know the perfect and acceptable will of God." The great issue is Conformity or Non-Conformity to the world, and that is what Protests are all about.

Unquestionably this is a time of protests, both profound and trivial. There is a new geography of protestations. Small towns have become milestones on the march of human progress, like Montgomery or Selma,

Alabama. Other sections of vast cities have been the scenes of violent protests, like Watts in Los Angeles or Harlem in New York City. Other places again have become merely bohemian havens of beatniks, like the Height-Ashbury district of San Francisco or Greenwich Village in New York City, where the beatniks have a new vocabulary in which cool cats find cheap pads to indulge in pot and acid. There have been many kinds of protests: protests for social justice; protests for academic justice in Berkeley, California and at St. John's in New York City; protests from labor strikes to the present landlords' strikes in Manhattan; there are military protests, and protests in support of our involvement in Vietnam. There are protests bohemian, and protests bourgeois.

Our age has been called many things from "the Aspirin Age" because of its headaches to the "Long Yawn" because of its boredom. I would suggest we call this decade the Button Age, because everyone seems to want to protest something.

Now what is to be our reaction to the phenomenon of protest? There are three attitudes:

1. The vast majority of persons are quite happy to be part of the undifferentiated masses, that is to take the balcony or television view of life and to point out how trivial and useless these protests are. You've heard the deprecatory words of the conformists: "They're just a bunch of beatniks; long-hairs; publicity-hounds; eggheads and addle pates; crazy bums with side-burns like wings, like that fellow Ginsberg and that other mad poet, Ferlinghetti or ... Is it Spaghetti?"

Such a view I frankly dismiss as far too superficial, because it is not even trying to distinguish the differences of the protests as between, say, Dr. Martin Luther King and Elijah Muhammad and Jack Kerouac—the one for integration by partnership, the second for violent racial segregation to be established by Black power, and the third a beatnik escapism from the struggle for Social Justice.

2. A second and very common university response is a much more Olympian version of the balcony, or spectator view of life. The essence of the university attitude is to cultivate objectivity in all controversial issues, for emotional involvement clouds the issues under discussion. Furthermore, science itself teaches to hold all conclusions tentative and temporary until proven or disproved by experiment. Even the careful scientist recalls that, as knowledge develops, radical revisions of every

hypothesis are required. Surely we must recognize how partial and relative all knowledge is?

With this I agree profoundly. It is excellent advice for the intellectual life, but it is dangerous advice for the moral and spiritual life where truth cannot be known except by commitment. I am alarmed when brilliant undergraduates think they are being scientific and cerebral when they play it cool, when they finesse on major moral and social issues. Above all, I am disturbed for the future when they develop what Professor Demos of Harvard has called a "commitment to non-commitment and a faith in non-faith."

I would shudder with horror if I thought that every graduate today was going to go out from this delightful island of academia to the mainland of the world, having decided that his commitment to the great issues of his time was to be minimal. I would regard his education as an almost total failure. For this superb training ground of engineers and others would have taught him mastery over nature only to leave him the slave of his own worst nature. I would not think him a man but only a chameleon, taking on the protecting coloring of his environment instead of a citizen challenging that environment.

Allow me to develop the grounds of my argument for a need for the increase of profound protests and protesters, for intelligent men who will speak out against the ills that damage the fabric of human society, and will be prepared to work and sacrifice for a more just society.

1. My first argument is the reminder that the mightiest religious leaders were, in fact, almost always God's angry young men. Moses, you will recall, faced the anger of proud Pharaoh, as he demanded with quiet wrath: "Let my people go." Amos, the countryman, shuddered as he saw the supinely affluent and uncompassionate society of Israel where they "joined field to field and house to house," while they sold the poor man for the price of a pair of shoes. Jesus, the great leader of Christians, was often gentle but once burning with savage indignation at the exploiters of the pious—the money-changers in the Temple; he impatiently overturned their tables, and cried: "You have turned the house of prayers for all nations into a den of thieves." I recall that St. Dominic, whose great Catholic order gave us the towering mind of St. Thomas Aquinas, pleaded with the thirteenth-century Pope of the day to allow him to start an Order dedicated to poverty, saying: "Because the Church can no longer say: 'Silver and gold have

I none,' neither can it say: 'In the name of Jesus of Nazareth rise up and walk.'"

And the very group of Christians who, in the year 1529, called themselves Protestants, did so at Speyer, because they dissented from Catholicism, believing that it had at that time overlaid the simplicities of the Gospel with a complex crust of tradition. And today true Catholics and true Protestants would reecho the words of the first Jewish disciples of Jesus: "We must obey God and not men." All these benefactors of the human race protested in the name of the Universal Father of mankind against the exploitation of his children, when thousands would have persuaded them that the eleventh commandment was: "Thou shalt not rock the boat!"

2. My second argument is a reminder that protest in the form of constant vigilance is the safeguard of freedom; and we pride ourselves above all else that America is the home of the free.

Can men with your heritage bear to see a race of Americans produced who will have their ears everlastingly to the ground, a race who will always be watching the facial expressions of others—especially those who can confer favors—a race fearful of every frown from those who can hire or fire them? Would you want to be an American quick to conform rather than to reform or transform? Would you rather take the easy path of comforting the afflicted rather than the challenging road of afflicting the comfortable?

Let us recall that America came into independence and power as she rallied free men to the burning slogan: "Rebellion to tyrants is obedience to God." America will remain free only if she believes with Emerson: "Whoso would be a man must be a nonconformist," or with John F. Kennedy: "The hottest places in Hell are reserved for those who in times of moral crisis preserved their neutrality."

The real issue for every Lehigh graduate today, as an inheritor of the values of the Judeao-Christian tradition, and as an American, is this: is his chief concern to be to acquire this world's goods, or to add to the world's good? If the aim is to be only acquisitive, it is the ambition of a hog, even if a degree adds two curly kinks to the pig's tail.

3. In the third place, however, we must try to distinguish between trivial and profound protests, between mere fads and fancies like beards and miniskirts, which are about as significant as the other eruptions of ado-

lescence like acne, and the great issues of the day such as war and peace, interracial justice, the ending of over-population and poverty.

The difficulty, as you will remind me, is that some protests are mixed. The Berkeley Free Speech Movement was certainly mixed. Along with a protest against the impersonality and lack of student-faculty contact in a vast university, there was an irresponsible demand for dirty speech as free speech, and a completely irresponsible demand to share in the control of the university on determining courses, and in the appointment and promotion of faculty. So I recognize that the issues must be analyzed and that irresponsibility has no rights.

On the issue of the present war in Vietnam there are no easy solutions. We do not live in the kingdom of heaven, but in a world of competing systems in which force must be returned with force. It is therefore the right of the nation to expect its young men to defend it wherever the nation thinks fit, and it is equally the right of draft boards to probe the motives of those who are conscientious objectors to war in general, or to the methods used in this war in particular. It is immensely hard to tell who sincere and courageous pacifists are and who mere skin-savers are. But I deeply admire the governments of the free world, because there is a place for truly conscientious objectors to military service.

There is one issue, however, on which we can all be fully committed: in the war against poverty the world over, and in the war in this land against racial injustice. The song of freedom in twentieth century America is unquestionably: "We shall overcome." And I would hope that every graduate of Lehigh will be found in that battle to guarantee the rights and dignities of every man, woman and child, regardless of race. There is nothing faddist or trivial about this protest. It is solemn, serious, and desperately important. For both religious and human reasons we have to banish from the face of the earth every racial and economic ghetto. The ultimate test of civilization is compassion.

I can assume that most university graduates are cultured; how I wish we could also assume that they were civilized, that is, that they combined, with their tough-mindedness in matters of the intellect, a sensitivity to the legitimate needs of others.

Let me conclude with a story that was told to me by a social welfare worker in South Africa. I lived in that land for six years where the racial problems are far more acute than in the deepest South of this country. This story is a parable. A pathetically poor and hungry African girl came to the welfare office for a glass of milk, her rickety limbs and her distended stomach proving she was a case of malnutrition. She was immediately offered a glass of milk. Before she allowed it to touch her lips, she glanced across at her younger brother, and she asked: "How far down may I drink?"

At this time, you will be drinking more interesting beverages than milk, perhaps the celebratory champagne. But as the goblet of opportunity is held in your hands, you must constantly ask, remembering the parched lips of God's underprivileged ones: "How far down dare I drink?"

28

Hoping against Hope

Preached at Westminster Abbey at Evensong,
Sunday, October 3, 1971
[with variants transcribed by this editor]

This is a recognition that hope has been shattered for modern man, but also that hope sprang from despair in many Biblical stories: the unexpected offspring of Abraham and Sarah and the Resurrection after the Cross. Out of the despair of Existentialism came a glimmer of hope in Camus's modest belief in human fellowship, whereas Communism attempted to find hope for the underprivileged. Bypassing God's alliance with his people, however, was bound to bring about the latter's failure. Here is a reaffirmation of the Judeo-Christian tradition, grounded in the Law, with the net, in case of failure, of the doctrine of the Resurrection and the restored Communion of Saints.

- Romans 4:18: "[Abraham] who in hope believed against hope to the end he might become a father of many nations."

"Hoping against hope." You have heard the phrase often enough and you may well know the experience of trying to be an optimist when pessimism seems more sensible. "Hoping against hope" is the faint hope of the cancer patient when he receives his first cobalt treatment. Or, it is the pale expectation of the university undergraduate who has little confidence in herself when she reads the first compulsory question in her first examination. "Hoping against hope" is humanity in the culture of today, with its gaping God-shaped blank, feeling orphaned in the universe; and what is left but to whistle in the dark to keep one's spirits up?

But—and this is very important—it was from this very situation that the community of faith was created, and from the experience of hoping against hope that Abraham became the first of the people of God.[1]

St. Paul reminds us in the fourth chapter of his great Letter to the Romans that when Abraham was a very old man with a barren wife, he was given the apparently ludicrous promise that he should be the father of many nations and that his seed should be more in number than the sand on the seashore. Here is St. Paul's interpretation of this seminal passage:

> Abraham ... who in hope believed against hope ... considered his own body as good as dead (he being about an hundred years old) and the deadness of Sarah's womb; yet looking unto the promise of God, he wavered not through unbelief, but grew strong in trust, giving glory to God, and being fully assured that what God had promised he was able to perform. (Romans 4:18–21)

You must swim against the engulfing black sea of contemporary existentialism, and you must swim against the red sea of revolutionary hopes.

The Existentialists are most brilliantly represented by the great French trio, Camus, Sartre and Sagan. Camus has written, among other works, *The Plague* (a novel about an epidemic that strikes the North African town of Oran), *The Stranger* and *The Fall*. Each shows man as the frustrated victim of circumstances too great for him to control, and their author, with tragic irony, died in an automobile accident. Jean-Paul Sartre conveys his nihilism admirably in the title of his play about Hell here on Earth, which is called *No Exit*. And Françoise Sagan has perfectly caught the mood in her novel, *Bonjour Tristesse* (*Welcome Sadness*).[2] They have considered the Christian hope and written it off as mere dreaming, sheer fantasy in cloud-cuckoo-land. They consider the world as a concentration camp and the task of moderately decent men and women is to improve the living conditions for the next batch of prisoners. Its creed is perfectly

---

1. Variant: This the very situation out of which the community of the faith was created; and it was the experience of the first of the faithful, Abraham, as St. Paul reminds us in the 4th chapter of the great Letter to the Romans.

2. Variant: One admires the courage with which they face "the slings and arrows of outrageous fortune," but this is a philosophy in which to die, not one by which to live. This is only to answer hope by despair, and where there is no hope, there is no point in living. We say: "Where's there's life, there's hope;" it would be equally true to say: "Where there is no hope, there is only death, for that's the way to death."

summed up in the warning of Albert Camus: "Our task is to think hard and not to hope."

In the brevity of a sermon, I can only say that they know the Cross experience, but not the Resurrection, the Fall of Man, but not the Rise of Man in the "Second Adam who to the fight and to the rescue came" and that they understand "*Bonjour Tristesse,*" but not "*Adieu Tristesse*" and "Hail gladdening Light . . ." Theirs is a brave Stoicism: a philosophy by which to die, but not a philosophy by which to live. The way of despair is the way of suicide, but the way of hope is the way of life.

The second group, the Marxist-Leninists, cannot be convicted of despair, but they can be criticized from the Christian standpoint of presumption and impatience. They cannot wait for God to bring in his Kingdom and City; they will anticipate him and establish the classless society.[3] As Moltmann has reminded us, the Existentialists picture man as the classical Sisyphus doomed everlastingly to roll a huge stone wheel up a hill which forever falls back on him; whereas the Marxists and Utopian idealists look to the daring Prometheus who stole fire from the Gods with Titanic impatience and pride.

One can understand the impatience that lies behind this view. It was that of the poor man in the mission hall who was sick of only being promised a heavenly crown at the end of a long and deprived life and he interrupted the preacher with his Cockney wit: "O for Gawd's sake, guvnor, give us 'alf a crown now." But we have seen so many revolutions followed by tyrannies: the France[4] of 1789 led to the Napoleonic dictatorship, and Moscow's liberation from the Czars was succeeded by the servitude of Hungary and Czechoslovakia. But Christian hope is not based on human social justice, though it is not contrary to it, and indeed hopes for it under the renovating power of God. But when all is said and done, the way of revolution is to be faulted on two accounts: it grossly underestimates the power of God, and it grievously overestimates the power of untransformed and unredeemed human justice and love.[5] As I rejected the despair of the

---

3. Margin note: John Steinbeck, *Tortilla Flat*—property, the cause of misery.

4. Variant: that William Wordsworth visited and of which he wrote soon after 1789: "France was standing on the top of golden hours and human nature seeming born again" led to the military dictatorship of Napoleon.

5. Variant: The way of revolution is to underestimate God's power and to overestimate man's justice. As I rejected the despair of the existentialists, I reject the impatience and presumption of the Revolutionaries.

Existentialists and Nihilists, so I also reject the presumption and pride of the God-playing Titanism of the Revolutionaries.

WHAT THEN, ARE THE GROUNDS FOR CHRISTIAN HOPE?[6]

1. The first and greatest ground of the Christian hope is the firmness of a promising and performing God. Zechariah could speak of the Jews exiled in Babylon and far from their native lands of Judah and Israel as "the prisoners of Hope."[7] Yes, and that the Messianic promise was fulfilled in Christ Jesus whom St. Paul called the "Yes," and "Amen" to God's promises. Abraham was justified in believing that "what God had promised, he was fully able to perform."

2. The second basis of trust in the Christian hope is the Resurrection of Jesus Christ from the dead.[8] Listen to the serene assurance in the words of 1 Peter 1:3: "Blessed be the God and Father of our Lord Jesus Christ! By his great mercy we have been born anew to a living hope through the resurrection of Jesus Christ from the dead."

"Wish fulfillment," you murmur under your breath. I deny it. When the disciples had seen Jesus crucified and buried, they thought the Christian enterprise was over.[9] They barricaded themselves behind closed doors and windows. They were the very image of black despair, afraid that a knock on the door would mean Roman soldiers taking them to their trials and probable crucifixions. Only the visitation of the risen Christ can explain the transformation of this defeated remnant into the spearhead of the noble army of martyrs. In Jerusalem, the place of defeat for him personally, St. Peter proclaimed the victorious truth: "This Jesus whom ye crucified, God hath made both Lord and Christ." God had promised that

---

6. Variant: How can we in this difficult time hope against hope?

7. Variant: There is a clue to be found in Zechariah's words about the Hebrew people, who were in abject slavery in Babylon, yet they were "the prisoners of hope." They believed that one day God would honor his promises by sending his own Deliverer, our Lord Christ, the hope of Israel.

8. Variant: The greater clue is from the coming of that deliverer and from his Resurrection. "Blessed be the God and Father of our Lord Jesus Christ! By his great mercy we have been born anew to a living hope through the resurrection of Jesus Christ from the dead." 1 Peter 1:3.

9. Variant: The disciples had gathered together in the Upper Room in Jerusalem where they barricaded . . .

his Holy One should not see corruption, and he kept his promise, and despair fled from the disciples like mists before the morning sun.[10]

3. The third ground for hope is the balance it gives to human life. My former teacher, Dr. Nathaniel Micklem, once put it this way. Because of the Cross, we can never be facile optimists, but because of the Resurrection we can never be deep pessimists. We are, therefore, Christian realists who have plumbed the depths and know the heights of human possibilities. This Christian hope is indeed a stabilizing anchor in the storms of life, and it means most assuredly that those who die in the Lord are forever Christ's. This is a conviction that is not only bracing, but also infinitely cheering because there are no limits to the preserving and providing love of God.

4. Lastly, it is in the strength of Christian hope that God's greatest saints and servants have lived and been sustained. Let me mention only one of them to whom the Church of England owed so much in its High Church renewal, in the years 1833 onwards, that blessed man, John Keble. His great sermon on "National Apostasy" started the Oxford Movement that returned reverence to divine worship throughout the English-speaking world, and beyond. In weather like this, he went up as a freshman to Oxford University and, of course, the journey was then by stagecoach. He chose to sit outside, bundled up from the cold, sitting beside the coachman. He fell asleep on this high perch and suddenly realized his danger as the coach rattled on the cobblestones of Oxford's High Street. For one moment that seemed an eternity, he thought that he would slip beneath the coach's wheels and be annihilated, and then he realized that the strong arm of the coachman was about him. He said, when he was a national figure afterwards, that he never thought of the great words of the Book of Deuteronomy that "underneath are the everlasting arms" of God, without interpreting them by the illustration of the coachman. They kept him from despair often when he was dispirited and downhearted, especially as he remembered that God had made the instrument of torture, the Cross, into the symbol of reconciliation, and the very grave not a terminus, but a tunnel to heaven.

---

10. Variant: The last word on human life is not that of cynical Pilate, nor of envious officialdom, nor of the fickle crowd, but the word of Christ as, expiring on the Cross, he cried: "Father into thy hands I commend my spirit." For God was faithful in fulfilling His promises. He was and He is.

These are some of the grounds of Christian hope and on that sure basis we may have confidence in life and death.[11]

"Now the God of Hope fill you with all joy and peace in believing, that you may abound in hope in the power of the Holy Spirit." And now to God the Father, God the Son . . .

---

11. Addition: By all means, work for human betterment. You can do so with all the more confidence because God has promised a new heaven and a new earth. His providence sees to it that the world is always renewing itself in youthful possibilities, and souls as well as the green earth can experience spring and the uncoiling of hope as vivid as ferns. But let your ultimate hope not be utopian, but theocentric, not man-centered but God-centered. And a hope that is fully "assured that what God has promised, He is fully able to perform." But also remember that God is not our grandfather which art in Heaven. He is "lightening and love," and often lightning before he is love.

Part Four

Jesus

Monarch of Men

29

Jesus Baptized

On one thing, all the Gospels are agreed. The call of Christ to his life's work was connected with John the Baptist's preaching and the whirlwind revival which that very preaching had started.

If we look at the situation, we can understand why John had to preach so sternly and why he had such crowds listening to him. The Jews of that day were a burdened people. They were heavily taxed by the Romans and equally heavily taxed by their own religious leaders. A man might have to pay as much as a third of his entire income to support the pagan Roman emperor and he might have to pay as much again to the Temple. Annas, and Caiaphas, his son-in-law, grew fabulously rich at the expense of the people. They practiced the most appalling extravagances in the Temple. They employed twenty thousand priests there alone.

The religious burden was heavier than the Roman taxation. The religious burden demanded scrupulous adherence to meaningless rules. To take one instance of this: some of the rules of the Sabbath. This meant not only must a man do no work in our sense on that day, but he must not wear artificial teeth, for that was carrying a burden; nor must he scrape a chair along the ground: that was ploughing, nor must a woman look at a mirror on the Sabbath lest, noticing a grey hair, she might pull it out; and that would be reaping. These very trivial instances should show how ridiculous the official practice of religion had become.

Against this John was passionately in revolt. He was no reed shaken in the wilderness; the popular breezes could not sway his iron-will. He criticized the Scribes and Pharisees to their faces. One day—this shows you the kind of man he was—one day as John was preaching, a company of the people near by had lit a fire to cook their meal on, when the bush above it caught fire. Instantly, scorpions, lizards and a brood of vipers rushed from underneath the bush to escape the flames. John's pointing finger shot out to a group of Pharisees standing near! "You brood of vipers, who warned you to flee from the wrath to come?... Bring forth the fruits of repentance, and do not say: 'We have Abraham for our father,' for out of these stones God can raise up children of Abraham."

If he was severe to the Pharisees, he was as ruthless to a king. Herod patronized him, and showered marks of favor on him. John was only a desert prophet; Herod was a ruler. It meant something to be flattered by a king. Surely the prophet would now be a little more careful in his speech, more apologetic, more ready to turn a blind eye to the king's private life? Will he indeed? Herod might be a king, but God was a King of kings. If the royal law of Heaven were broken, then straight into Herod's presence, John would go, with flashing eyes, and pointing finger and blunt rebuke: "It is not lawful for thee..." King or no king, you have no right to do it.

F. W. H. Myers's lines are a true picture of John the Baptist:

> John, than which man a grander or a greater
> Not till this day has been of woman born;
> John like some iron peak by the Creator
> Fired with the red glow of the rushing morn.
> If that was the man, then these lines describe his message:
> Also of John a calling and a crying
> Rang in Betharaba, till strength was spent,
> Cared not for counsel, stayed not for replying,
> John had one message for the world: "REPENT."

The voice of prophecy had been silent in Israel for two hundred years, and John's straightforward speaking had a tremendous impression. By and by the news of revival reached the market place in Nazareth and someone carried the news to a humble workshop where a carpenter was toiling at his bench; and Jesus knew that God's hour had struck, that the sign he had been waiting for was come. The very same day he rose and went.

What was Jesus's attitude to John to be? Three reactions were possible:

1. For one thing Jesus might easily have stood aloof. He might easily have told himself: this was a baptism of confession and repentance. He had nothing to confess or repent. Why should he go? For the others, deep-dyed in their sins it might be a Heaven-sent blessing; but not for him.

2. Again he might have challenged or criticized him. John's Gospel was so obviously imperfect; indeed it was only a half-gospel. Ought Christ

to countenance it? There were two defects in it that he saw. Firstly, it was terribly negative. John's followers, as Jesus said, were like children in the market-place playing at funerals, but his wanted to dance. The very fact that John was a desert-man, a hermit, told against him. He had missed the rapturous, radiant view of God for which Jesus stood. Robert Louis Stevenson wrote to his father: "I'll think more of your prayers, when I see more of your praises." That was where John came short with his "Thou shalt not."

Moreover Jesus saw that it was a religion built upon fear. Its theme was: "Flee from the wrath to come!" Is fear a fit weapon for driving men into religion? John was preaching a flaming God and Jesus longed to preach a Father God; ought Jesus to have opposed him?

Andrew Bonar and Robert Murray McCheyne were walking together one day. "McCheyne asked me," said Bonar, "what my last Sabbath's subject had been." It had been: "The wicked shall be burned into Hell." On hearing this awful text, he asked: "Were you able to preach it with tenderness?" There was too little tenderness in the Baptist's preaching, too much flame and denunciation. And Jesus might have refused to identify himself with it.

3. There was a third possible attitude and Jesus took it. He did not stand aloof nor did he oppose; but he accepted John. In the great humility of God's only Son, he went to John: "Sir, I would fain be baptized of thee."

Probably it was late in the evening that it happened. The crowds were dispersed; the Baptist weary and spent was left alone in prayer. Through the gloaming came a solitary figure, bronzed and young and clean. And when the Baptist, rising from his knees, met him, and looked into his face, he saw shining from out from the eyes of him a light he had never seen before: "very God of very God." When he heard the request "I would be baptized of thee," suddenly the suitability struck him. "I have need to be baptized of thee, and comest thou to me?"

But the quiet voice answered: "Suffer it to be so now. For thus it becometh us to fulfill all righteousness." And with that they went down into the water together and there happened the event which even angels might desire to look into: a man baptizing his Lord.

THE INNER MEANING OF THE BAPTISM OF JESUS

Some people have suggested that because this was a baptism of repentance, Jesus must have felt that he himself, like all his brothers on earth, had something to repent of. But since all his other prayers assume a perfect obedience to God, this answer will not do. We must look for other reasons if we are to understand the Baptism.

1. Firstly, Jesus was moved to act as he did because he felt a real debt to John. Here was a nation-wide religious revival; young and old had begun to take religion seriously. Men were at long last actually worrying about their sins. Now, defective as John's message was, it had given Jesus an enormously hopeful atmosphere in which to begin his work. John was a true forerunner. We may well believe that when Jesus offered himself for baptism, he did so partly from recognition that he owed a debt to his predecessor and from recognition that this revival that had been sweeping the land was a real movement of the Spirit of God.

2. He also had another motive. He went into Jordan to take his stand by the side of sinful men and women. This was a great redeeming act of self-identification. It pointed to the years to come when the Lord of glory should earn the nickname of "Friend of publicans and sinners," when he should go "wherever need called, reckless of reputation, to sit often at outcasts' tables, and to die at last between two thieves." He was numbered with the transgressors. True, but he numbered himself with them first of all.

So the Baptism of Jesus at Jordan points to the fact that the only love which possesses redeeming power is a love that goes all the way and identifies itself with others. So did Moses in the day of the people's sin and cried: "Blot me, I pray thee, out of thy book of life which thou hast written."

So St. Paul lamenting the blindness of his nation, exclaimed: "I could wish that myself were accursed from Christ for my brethren, my kinsman according to the flesh." So Father Damien's self-identification meant literal leprosy: "Whenever I preach to my people," were his words, "I do not say 'my brethren' as you do, but 'we lepers.'" It is of that self-identifying love of which the Baptism of Jesus speaks.

In the great moment of his Baptism, two things came to him: a voice and a vision.

The voice was the call for which through the silent years of Nazareth he had been waiting for—the call to his life's work: "This is my beloved Son in whom I am well-pleased." That swept the last hesitation from his soul and his great vocation was accepted.

The vision showed the heavens torn from end to end in a dazzling coruscation of light: this, the blazing majesty of God was succeeded by a quieter vision of the Spirit of God as a descending on the waters.

The voice was the call and the encouragement of God; the vision of the Spirit was the equipment for carrying out the work.

After seeing the vision and hearing that voice, the carpenter of Nazareth came up from the waters of Baptism as the Messiah, the Called of God and as the power of God unto salvation. To whom be all glory and praise, dominion and might, now and for ever more.

30

Jesus the Evangelist

Every new idea that has ever burst into the world has had a watchword. It has always had a slogan to emblazon on its banners, as it went marching through the world.

Islam had its watchword: "God is God and Mohammed is his prophet." The French Revolution had its motto: "Liberty, Equality, and Fraternity." The democratic ideal had its slogan: "Government of the people, by the people, for the people."

The greatest idea ever born had its own watchword, coined by the Master. It was an impressive summary of his message. The watchword was: "The Kingdom of God."

Every great leader who has ever risen among the sons of men has been dominated by a master-thought. It has gripped the man like a passion, burning in his sky like the Greenland sun, never setting night or day. Socrates had a master-thought: the immortality of the soul. Buddha had a master-thought: the renunciation of the world. Napoleon had a master-thought: the dominion of Europe. Now the greatest Leader who has ever led the hosts of humanity is Jesus Christ, and like the other leaders he brought his master-thought, world-shaking and world-transforming: "the Kingdom of God."

In the Gospels, the name "Kingdom of God" occurs over a hundred times. His first sermon had as its theme: "The time is fulfilled: the Kingdom of God is at hand." (Mark 1:15) The last sermon of his earthly ministry had the same great theme. When Jesus returned to his own after Calvary, according to the Book of Acts, he spoke to them "of the things pertaining to the Kingdom of God" (Acts 1:3).

If this note was struck at the beginning and at the end of his ministry, it resounded throughout. How many parables begin: "The kingdom of God is like . . ." Remember also his commission to his disciples: "Into whatsoever city ye enter, say unto them: 'The Kingdom of God is come nigh unto you.'" This is undoubtedly the master-thought of his life. Or, to put it another way, it is the theme on which all his other sayings are variations.

WHAT DID HE MEAN BY "THE KINGDOM OF GOD"?

It is first of all important to remember that if the idea was original in Jesus, the name was not. In the generation immediately before Jesus two things had happened to the Jewish idea of the Kingdom of God. First, it had redoubled in intensity. That was the direct result of the Roman domination; for, with the Roman heel pressing on the throat of Israel, the only hope was that God would strike in, and make his Kingdom come. In the second place, the idea of God's kingdom had become materialized and secularized. Material splendors, political advantages, secular benefits, these were the objects of the popular hopes. Even the men that Jesus chose found it hard to break from the prevailing secularism. You remember that James and John asked for the best places in the Kingdom, and even after the Resurrection, the disciples asked: "Lord wilt thou at this time restore again the Kingdom to Israel?" In fact, the Kingdom of God had come to be the slogan of Jewish nationalism.

We know how strong the nationalist spirit can be. We think of Mazzini in Italy, Sun-yat-sen in China, or Gandhi in India, each of them fanning the nationalist spirit into a blaze. Never in the whole course of history has the nationalist spirit been stronger than in the Israel of our Savior's day. Jewish nationalism had even entrenched itself in the Temple, the very last place where it should have intruded. There, between the outer court of the Gentiles and the inner court of the Jews, stood a barrier with this written on it: "Let no foreigner enter within. Whosoever is arrested doing so, will himself be the cause of the death that overthrows him."

Now Jesus took the conception of the Kingdom of God and transformed it almost beyond recognition. Its new meaning was as majestic as it was simple. It proclaimed that man's life consisted in a two-fold attitude. Man "could look up into the face of God and say 'my Father,' and he could stretch out his hand to every one of his fellows, of whatever nation, or kindred or tribe, or tongue and say 'my brother'" (Leslie Weatherhead's words).

In other words, Jesus thought of the Kingdom of God in two ways. First it was the rule of God in the heart. Secondly it was the rule of God in the world. Let us look at these two aspects separately.

THE KINGDOM AS THE RULE OF GOD IN THE HEART.

How this simple profound message has been overlaid. Look at some aspects of our modern Christianity and ask yourself whether we are conveying the simple good news of Jesus. Here is one man who says, smiting the cover of the Bible: "I believe in this infallible book from the first word in Genesis to the last word in Revelation. There is not a single mistake in history or science or fact." And one recalls that Jesus himself made a very careful selection of the Books of the Old Testament. He clearly did not believe they were all equally inspired; and one remembers that this book was written by scores of different writers over a period of some thousand years and more. Here is another man, and he says: "I belong to an infallible Church which, through its Pope, has never made a mistake in theology or morality." Here is another one who says: "Unless you are baptized by total immersion in water, you have no right to be considered a Christian." Here is another who claims that a true follower of Christ must attend a particular service at eight o'clock in the morning, because it has extraordinary virtue and piety at that time, but if it is held at eight o'clock in the evening, it is valueless. He would refuse to partake of the sacramental meal if the bread were passed to him by some saintly layman. He would accept it only from the hands of a man who put forward the claim that he was in the apostolic succession of St. Peter. Here is another person who restricts discipleship to the recitation of an intellectual creed which only a person with a special theological training could even understand, let alone subscribe to. Jesus stands among us, tied up in our formalism, our conventions, our creeds and rituals and superstitions, our hymn-drugged souls, and our retreats from life and says: "Follow me."

Jesus brought good news. In the Old Testament, God was like a Father, but very rarely. At other times he was a fierce, jealous, avenging deity who would drown the Egyptians, leave thousands of the Assyrians dead on these shores, and demand the first-born of his own chosen people unless there was a blood-smear on the pillar of the house. To touch his ark meant death. He would lead his people if they behaved themselves, but if not, he cursed them with plagues, lice and frogs and boils, and poisoned rivers. What a God!

Turn from such a grim picture to the story of the Prodigal Son. "And when he was afar off, his father saw him, and was moved with compassion and ran and fell on his neck and kissed him." What good news indeed! What an incentive to change your way of looking upon life and thus enter into a fellowship with all God's sons and daughters, and living the life of fellowship, bring in the reign of God, the kingdom of right relations! Why, it is tremendous news. Loved by God for ever with a strong, tender, [and] everlasting love! The foulest can be made clean again, can lift his head, and begin again. He also is a son of God. A new way of life opened in those far-off days, which has changed the face of the world. Where is the church of God in Scotland at this day?

THE KINGDOM ALSO MEANT THE RULE OF GOD IN THE WORLD

A young communist poet at Cambridge went out to Spain to fight against the Fascists and lost his life there. After his death, a book of essays written by him was published. He had been looking for a great loyalty to which he could attach himself. He first turned towards Christianity before accepting communism. "But," he said: "I found that most Christians were only interested in saving their own souls." Religion—God's kingdom—begins in my heart and yours, but it only begins there. It continues and ends as God's rule in the world. It is the realm of Right Relationships.

When Jesus told his men of their high responsibility as Christians, he said: "Ye are the salt"—of what? Not of the Church, not of their own families, not of any one class, or sect, or party: "Ye are the salt of the earth."

Never did Jesus think of God's kingdom as an ark of refuge for the few, to which they could escape with a sigh of relief from the ruined world. Any church content to minister to the few who are saved already is failing Christ. The Church is here under Christ to claim nothing less than the whole world for God's kingdom. It is here to cleanse politics and social life, to redeem a national life and to unite the world in the removal of all barriers to fellowship.

The Kingdom is only in its beginnings. It is here now wherever there is a fully surrendered heart, but its crowning glory is yet to come. Jesus said: "When the Son of man shall come in his glory, then shall the King say: 'Come ye, blessed of my Father, inherit the Kingdom.'"

Whatever else? That mighty Second Advent hope that glowed and blazed in Jesus's heart may mean—it does at least mean this: that when man has done everything that man can do to build the everlasting Kingdom, it is God, and God alone, who can make that Kingdom perfect. That somehow and somewhere, in ways beyond our present comprehension, God is going to come, breaking in triumph. That the age-long warfare between good and evil is not to drag on indefinitely, but that one day it is going to end, and end in the victory of God. That was the winning note that that Jesus struck. He believed that one day, heaven itself would ring with a mighty tumult of voices, and their adoring rejoicing cry would be this: "The kingdoms of this world are become the kingdom of our Lord and he shall reign for ever and ever."

Is this merely a Utopian dream? No. Look at Matthew, selling his birthright to the hated foreigner. Look at his hard face and cynical mouth. Jesus says: "Follow me!" and he comes. St. Matthew? Why? How? How in the world? "He did it," says Matthew. "He showed me a new world and then brought me into it, and I was glad to die for him at last." He did it, that is the refrain through the centuries? Of course he can change persons. Can he change nations? Yes he can even do that.

In South America, nations had been at war for centuries. Then, one day, they signed a treaty pledging themselves to peace in the name of the Prince of Peace, to show their earnestness. They constructed a metal statue of our Savior from the armament with which they had attacked one another and placed it on their frontier. Its inscription said: "At the feet of the crucified Christ, we pledge ourselves never to fight again, as long as the Andes shall last."

31

Jesus, Social Thinker

Preached March 7, 1943

Did Jesus preach a social Gospel? Was he interested in bettering the social conditions of men? If you had put this question to a mediaeval monk, he could have answered it with an abrupt: "No." Indeed, I doubt if you would ever have put the question to him. See him in his cold, cheerless cell, whose darkness is pierced by a spear of light that comes through his narrow slit of a window. Notice his rough grey cassock with the roughest cord. Picture his lean cadaverous face, made thin by fasting and prayer. Do not neglect the human skull that grins at him from the wall, a permanent reminder of our mortality. If you had seen all that, it could have made the question irrelevant. Clearly his whole life was based on the belief that Christ demanded renunciation of the world. He, at least, was certain that Christ came not to save the world as it was, but to save men out of the world.

The early persecuted Christians in the catacombs of Rome would have said the same as they mumbled their agonizing prayer: "Come, Lord Jesus, come."

Our Puritan forefathers would have given the same answer. Christ said: "Come out and be separate."

For at least the first seventeen centuries of the Christian era, Christians were the men with the upturned eyes, pagans the men with downcast eyes. The Christian was more interested in heaven, the pagan more interested in earth.

Even today the mistaken view is held by some of our most eminent thinkers that Jesus was quite unconcerned to change the conditions of men. Dr. C. E. M. Joad in a book published only a few months ago writes: "So far as Jesus himself is concerned, we search his sayings in vain for any statement on art, music, science, or philosophy, while problems of sexual relationship, of politics and economics are to all intents and purposes ignored." You will find that on page 22 of his book, *God and Evil*.

I challenge that statement. I grant that Jesus makes no statements on art or music; he was not an artist or a musician and we don't expect such statements from him. But it is a gross exaggeration to say that he was disinterested in philosophy. If philosophy be (as the Oxford dictionary defines it) a study of ultimate reality, what else is his teaching and life but a study of ultimate reality? It is equally untrue to say that Jesus made no pronouncement on sex. What of the woman taken in adultery? What of the beatitude: blessed be the pure in heart? As to politics—the art of the government of men—did he not say in answer to a political problem: "Render unto Caesar the things of Caesar and unto God the things of God"? Isn't the Sermon on the Mount deeply concerned with economics?

I want to show that Jesus had a defined attitude to social problems. He throws light on three great social issues:

1. How men should live together; 2. The right attitude to poverty; 3. The individual's duty to the state.

HOW MEN SHOULD LIVE TOGETHER

The first thing that Jesus did was to give family life a deeper significance. He lived for the greater part of his life in a family. He had four brothers and at least two sisters. For thirty years the glorious Son of God was content to dwell in a peasant's home. That has hallowed family life for ever.

Indeed as a proof of the importance he attached to family life, we see that he regarded the family as a miniature of the life of the Kingdom of God. From the family, he drew his picture of God. God, he said, is a Father. The greatest of all the parables—that of the Prodigal Son—is a picture of home life. Forgiveness as experienced in the home is a fine clue to understanding the forgiveness of God. The family was a mirror of the Kingdom of God on a wider scale.

Thirdly, most of all, Jesus defended the sanctity of family life by what he did for women and children. Here we have to go on his whole attitude rather than on his teaching. The Jews were great upholders of the family, but the man was the master; the woman was the slave. Unfaithfulness in the woman was not met by forgiveness on the part of the husband. No, he gave her a bill of divorce. Jesus set a higher value on women. In marriage both contracting parties were equal. Jesus said: "Whom God hath joined together, let no man put asunder." Paul was true to his Master in saying that in Christ there is no distinction between male and female.

He also raised the status of children. You can best understand the difference that the coming of Christ made in the treatment of children by comparing his attitude with that of this letter. It is written by a husband on foreign service to his wife at home. Its exact date is 1 BC, he says: "Let me tell you that we are still in Alexandria. I beg of you to look after the child and, as soon as we get wages, I will send you something. If it is a boy, let it alone, if it is a girl, throw it away."

Compare that callous picture with the account of Jesus calling the little child and setting him in the midst, and saying: "And who so shall receive one little child in my name receiveth me... But who so shall offend one of these little ones... it were better for him that a millstone were hanged around his neck and that he were drowned in the depth of the sea" (Matthew 18). Into a world that looked upon children merely as animals to be fed until they reached maturity and could be useful, or killed off if they were puny or females, into such a world, Jesus gave childhood a new importance. Of such is the kingdom of God.

THE RIGHT ATTITUDE TO WEALTH AND PROPERTY

It is surprising how many of the parables of Jesus allude to money matters. The parable of Lazarus, the poor man, and Dives, the rich man; the Hidden Treasure; the Unmerciful Servant; the two Debtors; the Good Samaritan; the Lost Coin and the Talents. Apart from parables, several important incidents concern money: for instance, consider the gift that the poor woman made to God and especially the interview of the rich young ruler with Jesus. Jesus was a realist, not a fanciful dreamer, dwelling on the clouds. He had to give men advice on the pressing problem of the right attitude towards money. His teaching is most valuable, even today.

He said that possessions in themselves are not necessarily wrong. He had one rich man in his circle of friends, Joseph of Arimethea, who built his sepulcher. He had many, who, if not wealthy, were well-to-do. Nicodemus, the centurion of Capernaum and the women who ministered unto him of their substance. When Jesus demands that the rich young ruler should give all his goods to the poor, he was not laying down a universal law. He was hitting at the one thing in this case that was blocking the road of that man's soul to the Kingdom. The moral of the tale of the rich man and Lazarus is not that the rich man was tormented for being rich, whilst the poor man went to heaven because he was poor. Lazarus was in Abraham's bosom in heaven and Abraham was one of the richest men the world has ever known. Possessions in themselves are not evil. So that Jesus does not condemn wealth and property outright.

Nor did he teach that poverty was a blessed thing. He was certainly poor. He was a homeless wanderer. He had to borrow even the coin he used for an illustration... When he died he left no possession except the robe he was led to Calvary in. They buried him in another man's tomb. The poverty of Jesus was voluntarily undertaken so that he might reach the lowest levels of society without embarrassing his hearers. It is very different from the squalid and degrading poverty of our modern industrial civilization. No glorification of its squalor can be found in the Gospels. The spirit of Christ is at work in the world to end such misery and to secure to every man the opportunity for fullness of life.

He also taught that possessions must be regarded as a sacred trust. Every man is accountable to God for the use he makes of them. We have received everything from God and we are all God's stewards. Nothing is more certain to bring condemnation, in God's judgment of the world, than a selfish attitude toward the good things of this life.

Again he insisted that if a man's possessions are beginning to injure his soul, drastic sacrifices are necessary. It is better to go into the kingdom of heaven a beggar, than to enter it a rich man with a beggared, shriveled soul: "What shall it profit a man if he gain the whole world and lose his own soul?" That is plain, common-sense teaching.

A RIGHT ATTITUDE TO THE STATE

Finally we turn to a very revealing incident. You must picture the jealous Pharisees try to trap Jesus into making false answers to a very difficult question. They want to discredit him. They bait the trap with flattery: "Master we know that thou art true and teachest the way of God with truth." Then they brought out their awkward question out: "Is it lawful to give tribute to Caesar or not? Ought we to pay the civil tax?" The trap had been laid with diabolic subtlety. If Jesus answered "Yes," then loyal Jews smarting under Roman taxation would be finished with him. If he said

"No," he would be charged with sedition by the Romans, and they would suppress him. If he kept silence, the people would assume he didn't know. If he hesitated, it would undermine his authority.

But Jesus broke through the trap. He said: "Show me the tribute money." When the coin was handed to him he declared: "Whose is this image and superscription?" "Caesar's," was the answer. "Render therefore to Caesar the things which are Caesar's and to God the things that are God's." Give to Caesar what belongs to him and to God what belongs to him.

He taught us two truths for our guidance:

1. Privilege carries obligations. Rights carry duties. If you are indebted to the State, then it is a moral duty to honor that debt. The State provides education, law, and order. Therefore it demands our loyalty. Duty is a sacred thing as many men are aware today who leave their home to defend the State and pay their debts to it, if need be, with their lives: "Render unto Caesar the things that are Caesar's."

2. Jesus also taught that as Caesar's image was on the coin, so God's image is on the soul. Through all the tangle and undergrowth of the vexed social question of his day, Jesus cuts down to eternal fact. He brings everything to personal surrender. You belong to God, he says, then honor your debt. Give God his due.

That is the heart of his teaching. Before God can put the world right, he must put you right. True happiness is not gained by a change of plan, but by a change of man. The beginning of the new order is not in a revived league of nations, or in a federal union, but in the new man. In you.

God grant that you may rise to this challenge: "Behold I make all things new."

32

Jesus, Man of Prayer

Preached March 21, 1943

I WAS STRUCK, THIS last week, by the extraordinary fuss we make about our religious doubts and difficulties. We parade our doubts in a kind of religious Ascot; the newer the fashion of the doubt, the more we are to be admired. Can you conceive of one woman saying to another: "You've only got arthritis, but I've rheumatism in every limb. What do you think of that? That's something to be proud of." We should think that a woman who said that had gone mad. Yet in the religious life we are all showing off about our doubts. That's what it comes to, an impudent display of diseases.

I was amazed by the contrast in the life of Jesus. He didn't argue about the existence of God. He simply trusted God. He didn't argue about the existence of a future life, he simply said: "God is a God of the living and not of the dead." He didn't discourse on the difficulties of prayer. He prayed. If we had only seen his transfigured face as he descended from Mount Hermon after a night in prayer, our doubts would be dispelled as surely as the morning sun drives away the mists from the mountainside.

In every sphere of life we trust the experts. If we call in the doctor, we obey his instructions implicitly. If we are involved in a legal case, we put our faith in the barrister we have briefed. Why then, when we have the advice of the expert in religion, Jesus Christ, must we forever be raising our amateurish doubts? By all means discover whether you can trust your expert, enquire into his qualifications, and seek testimonials of others who know him. Then, when you have ascertained the worth of the doctor or the barrister, leave the rest to him. In the same way, prove up to the hilt that the preaching and practice of our Savior are consistent. Seek the testimony of the religious leaders of the world—St. Paul, St. Francis, Luther, and Brother Lawrence—whom you will. But when you have their unanimous testimonial to the supreme qualifications, cease your questionings. To continue to doubt is then mere petulance and querelousness. Once you have their verdict, "trust and obey, for there's no other way," as the old hymn reminds us.

This morning come with faith and trust and watch the kneeling figure of the Messiah to see what he can teach you about the life of prayer. He will teach us three things.

1. We must engage in prayer before all the most important undertakings of life.

The first thing we notice about Jesus is that he was found praying in all the important crises of his life.

He prayed about his life's calling: "It came to pass" says St. Luke, "that Jesus being baptized, and praying, the heaven was opened and the Holy Ghost descended."

He also prayed for guidance. When he had to make the momentous decision of choosing who were to be his life companions, he spent this whole night in prayer. St. Luke informs us: "He went out into a mountain to pray and continued all night in prayer to God."

Last Sunday we saw that his disciples failed to cure a particularly baffling case of demon possession. "Why could we not cast it out?" they asked Jesus. The answer was: "This kind can go forth by nothing but by prayer." There we see Jesus praying for strength for his mighty works.

Then there came a day when the dark shadow of the Cross loomed large above him. And the temptation to evade it came upon him in the unstriped glade of Gethsemane. "Being in an agony," says the evangelist, "he prayed." There you see him praying against temptation.

Finally, there came an hour when the nails and the torture of Calvary had almost completed their ghastly work. All strength was ebbing away and the chill waters of Jordan seemed to roll about his feet. "Father" cried Jesus, "into thy hands I commend my spirit." There you see the Jesus who died praying.

At all the great crises of his career, you find the Master at prayer. The disciples had asked Jesus to teach them to pray. Here was his answer. He gave the pattern not only to his first disciples, but also to his latest disciples. Crises such as these through which he prayed, come to all of us. The true disciple will pray at the opening of his life's work; he will pray in all life's momentous decisions; he will pray for strength to do the works of God; he will pray for victory when temptation assaults him; he will pray when the shadows of the valley of death begin to curtain him around. Every hour of crisis will find him, as it found his Master, with bent knees and uplifted soul. He will be, as Tennyson finely describes it, "battering the gates of Heaven with storms of prayer."

2. Prayer was the habitual atmosphere of his daily life.

He prayed habitually. You can see the evidence of this in almost every page of the Gospels. We find Jesus rising up in the early morning to pray while the entire world was still asleep. "A great while before day," says St. Mark.

You find him praying, after an exhausting day's toil, keeping watch with God throughout the night.

You find him surrounded with crowds who broke in greedily upon his privacy and clamored for his help. Yet even in these surroundings, he clutches God's hand for a moment in prayer. Prayer, as any of the disciples would have told, was not merely an important part of his life. It *was* his life [and] the very air that he breathed.

This fact ought to rebuke us for our slipshod attitude to prayer. It means that all those things that thwart and stifle our prayer-life had no power with the Lord.

For instance we are often at the mercy of moods. He most certainly had changes of feeling: he smiled and he sorrowed; he was exhilarated and he was weary. But as the compass turns north, his heart turned to prayer. Jesus loved God his Father so utterly and so passionately that he could not bear to be away from him. He used every opportunity. The nights and days brought him to go and speak to God.

It really means for us that those failures in our prayer-life which we trace back to lack of mood are signs of something more serious. They are symptoms of a breakdown of affection.

What also stifles prayer for us is pressure of work or busyness. We claim that the days are so full that prayer is crowded out. Sometimes we even insist that work is prayer itself. But look at Jesus. Busy and crowded as our days are, his were more so. Think of the pressure of work in his case. Sick people and broken sinners came clamoring for him until late in the night and he refused none of them. There was a whole world to be redeemed and he was the only Redeemer. There was a thorough-going revolution in the minds and morals of men to be worked out, and he had only his own body and soul as the instruments of that revolution. Yet the world's greatest toiler was its greatest mystic. However busy he was, he found time to shut the door and kneel. How shabby our excuses seem in the light of his practice.

But the most serious difficulties that impede our prayers are moral difficulties. Communion with God inevitably grows artificial and unreal, if there is in our own lives some decision we are not prepared to face. The first necessity for prayer is a background of absolute moral honesty. Only the pure in heart can see God. Electricians speak of certain objects as insulators. They mean that these automatically break the contact and cut off the current. Sin is the most serious insulator that breaks off our prayer contact with God. The Psalmist says truly: "If I regard iniquity in my heart, the Lord will not hear me." This is the root of most of our troubles in prayer. We cannot conscientiously ask God's guidance again since we have refused it in the promptings of our consciences. There lies the difference between Jesus and ourselves. He obeyed and could seek for guidance.

3. The secret of our Lord's prayer-life is found in his ultimate knowledge of God.

Suppose you had someone seriously ill at home, and, for that person's recovery, it was essential to obtain eggs and butter. Would you ask complete strangers for their rations? If you did, you would you suggest it with much hope of receiving the reply you wanted. No, in that crisis you would turn either to a neighbor you knew very well or to a friend.

So it is with your prayers. Your prayers are not effective if they are directed to God the stranger. But they are powerful if you are addressing God the friend, or God the neighbor. The secret of Christ's prayers was the simple fact that he was speaking to God the friend. To speak to God more simply and naturally, you must know him more intimately.

Jesus has filled in for us the perfect portrait of God. He is the Father of our Lord Jesus Christ. He saw God in three ways and this produced the radiant faith and trust in God.

God was for him first the all-operative God. He knew for a certainty that behind and beyond all things lie not a dead soulless piece of mechanism, not any kind of fate blindly working to natural laws, but absolute life and spirit. "With God all things are possible," he said. God is for him absolute free-will. Before him every other power and will are as dust. There are no limits to the love and power of God. Whoever has faith in this absolute power and staggers not shall say to this mountain: "Be taken up and cast thyself into the sea" and it shall be done. God is the all operating, here and now at work in the world.

God was also the all-holy. So religion is utter obedience to the demands of God. For Jesus there is no halfway house between the good and the evil. The publicans and sinners whom he loves are real sinners, not decent people, dragged down by their environment. The Prodigal Son is a real prodigal, not a good guy who made a slight mistake. Jesus sees everything in black and white because he sees it as from the eyes of the all-holy God. Because God is absolutely holy, religion involves merit and reward, demerit and punishment, Heaven and Hell. He sees clearly the absolute antithesis between good and evil, because his standard is the abiding vision of Holy God.

Finally, he also sees God as infinitely gracious. He is all-powerful, all-holy, but all-loving too. The moment man repents the Father will take back the Prodigal Son and put the festal robe on him.

From this three-fold picture of God comes the vital courage and confidence of Jesus. From it springs his prayer life. Know God and you will pray to him in faith, nothing wavering.

33

Jesus Enthroned

Preached May 9, 1943

In his *Autobiography* Chesterton tells the following story. A solemn friend of his father used to go for walks on Sunday, carting a prayer-book, without the least intention of going to church. He calmly defended it by saying, with uplifted hand, "I do it, Chessie, as an example to others."

We are not, of course, hypocrites of that order, even if we have unused Bibles occupying a prominent place on our bookshelves. But our hypocrisy is of a subtler kind. We approve of Christianity for the "backward" races; we approve of Christianity as a moral dynamic for the degraded and the debauched; we approve of Christianity as a means of character-building amongst the young. We support the London Missionary Society. Well . . . we give a few passing thoughts and pence to our City Missions and the Salvation Army. Very occasionally we attend the open meetings of our Young People's Fellowship. In other words, we think Christianity has a message for the heathen, the down-and-out, and the young. We even pay other people to get on with the job. But has Christianity a message for us? I very much suspect that we might say: "I do it for the sake of others."

We have been considering for a good many Sundays the Life of our Lord, starting from his birth, and today we come to the climax of the series: Jesus enthroned. We shall be singing soon: "Jesus shall reign wher-e'er the sun / doth his successive journeys run," a fine hymn wedded to royal tune. But will it mean anything to us? How can Christ be enthroned in the world until he is enthroned as sovereign Lord in our hearts.

My theme is the enthronement of Christ. All that I have told you on previous Sunday mornings is only the first installment of the triumph of Christ. It was a tremendous triumph. The full price of sin was paid; the revelation of redeeming love was perfect and complete. Beyond Jesus we need not hope to go. But the Christ of history must become the Christ of the world. That story is the second volume: it is the never-ending story of the conquests of Christ and we are the living epistles that help to make up that comprehensive volume.

I want us to try and recapture the early enthusiasm of the first disciples whose passion it was to make Christ King. Four things drove them to do it. And, even in our altered circumstances, the same four incentives should drive us as goads and spurs to win the world to the sovereignty of the Savior.

1. First there was the *command of Jesus* himself. "All power is given unto me in heaven and earth. Go ye therefore and teach all nations." St. Luke tells us that when Jesus gave his followers the commission, he added the words: "Beginning at Jerusalem." That is a most illuminating thought. It suggests that a man's witness to Christ ought to start right on the very spot where he happens to be. Jerusalem was the scene of the disciples' shameful desertion of their Master in his hour of need; and in the very same place they were to stand up for him before the eyes of all men.

This Christian service is a command. Christ does not ask his followers as a favor to bear witness to him amongst men. He claims it as a duty: "Ye are my friends, if ye do whatsoever I command you" (John 15:14). Christ does not want fair weather friends, who come like flies to buzz around in smiling sunny weather, but who rush back to their hiding-places as fast as their wings can carry them in the cold and the rain. "Christianity does not mean complimenting Christ as genius, or artist, or teacher," says the Reverend J. S. Stewart, "It means bowing to Christ as Commander."

I have by now lost patience with people who say that they see no reason why the Church of Christ should go propagating its faith to the ends of the earth, while there is so much to do at home. Two facts are the final answer to that objection. The first is that a religion that does not propagate itself dies. The second is that the Lord himself has settled this question once and for all in his command: "Go ye therefore and teach all nations." The man who presumed to argue about this is daring to correct Jesus Christ. The Master's ruling has been given. He means it to be obeyed.

2. The second factor that compelled the disciples to witness for Christ was the *urgency of the situation*. They were convinced that the end of the world was at hand. It might even happen in their own life-time. The King's business required haste. Men were everywhere sitting in darkness and in

the shadow of death, hopeless and godless, lost and ruined. Christ's men were driven forth to preach by the very urgency of the situation.

This factor lays a duty upon their successors. To gloss over the present situation, with pretty platitudes and over-weaning optimism, is not the way that Christ's men and women can best serve him.

Three quarters of Europe is engulfed with a new and deadly paganism. Our men are doing their utmost by their bodies to hold the dykes of Christendom from this dark and ruinous flood. But they are only making possible the opportunity for the greater proclamation of the Gospel of Christ. The vast majority of our valiant defenders are decent, reliable, and courageous; but they are not Christians.

The French have a word, *déraciné*, that means uprooted. They use that word to describe a country which is living on the sustenance of the immediate past. That word describes the condition of the English people today. We are the uprooted people. Our fathers had roots firmly embedded in the Christian faith; but we are uprooted and, if Christianity shows some green foliage even today, it comes from the stored nourishment in the roots, not from the soil. We have also been called the men of the twilight; the sun of Christianity has set in Europe and a few rays still glimmer on in this country. But we are rapidly approaching the twilight and the midnight hour of blackness. Whether the dark ages will succeed, or a dawn of a more vigorous Christianity, depends upon God and us.

That is the urgency of our situation. In this emergency we have all to become preachers of the relevance of Christ to the Age. More witness, deeper integration of Religion to life and society and war are called for. This is a day when every man who has been with Jesus and believes in Jesus, should himself feel, by the very urgency of the situation, ready to witness to Jesus in the world.

3. The third incitement was the very *grandeur of the message*. Christ's religion spoke of the arms of God around the raggedest and muddiest souls of every class and every nation. It taught men to laugh in the face of death. It was victory over the enemies of man: sin, suffering and death. The good news had to be advertised.

There is an old Greek proverb which says: "Those who have the light must pass on the torch." Every man today who once grasps the truth knows that the most glorious and essential thing in the world is to be a herald and an ambassador. "Woe is me if I preach not the Gospel." cried St. Paul. "It is the power of God unto salvation." We have seen the light, the light that lighteth every man coming into the world. We can also see the danger-light that dominates the crossroads of our time. The glory of the message demands that it be proclaimed by us.

4. Lastly, the disciples are sent out by the conviction that *Jesus is Lord*. This was embodied in the earliest Christian creed. The Christians who used this title meant by it that the Friend to whom they owed everything would be one day the Judge of the World. All the kingdoms of this world would be his, and he would be Lord indeed. It means that the throne of the Universe belongs to Christ. Daring as his claim is, we who know Christ know that he has a right to it. It has been bought with a price. Bought with the hunger in the desert; bought with the tears he shed over the sons of men; bought with the sweat of Gethsemane; bought with the Cross that broke his body in death; bought with the deathless love that through the years still refuses to let a lost world go. The Captain of humanity has himself been in the ranks. If he rides at the head of the Host, it is because he once trudged in the mud, as foot-soldier. If he is to be King over the sons of men, it is because of what he has suffered for men. "Wherefore," says St. Paul, "God also hath highly exalted him and given him a name that is above every name." Our instinct is right that his Kingdom cannot fail.

It is true that Jesus shall reign. The Christ of History shall be the Christ of the Universe. Already we see him standing where the roads of class meet. General Booth of the Salvation Army used to say that no man's arms were long enough to reach out and give a hand to rich and poor alike. Human arms may not do it, but the Divine arms that were stretched wide on Calvary can.

Jesus is standing where the roads of great thinking meet. The literature of mankind has been haunted by the fascination of the Kingly Christ. Dante and Milton have written deathless epics of his story. Once the titans of British and American literature met. Carlyle was host to Emerson at Carlyle's Scottish home. As they walked together over a hill, the little village church came in view beneath them. Carlyle stopped and, turning to Emerson, he said: "Christ died on the tree that built Dunscore Kirk yonder; that brought you and me together!"

Jesus is standing at the roads where religion meets. Just before the outbreak of this war, a great gathering of young Christians under thirty-five met together at Amsterdam, representatives of many nations. The motto of their conference emblazoned on an immense banner in the Conference Hall was *Christus Victor,* Christ the Conqueror.

Jesus shall reign; make no mistake. But shall we suffer with him, so that we shall reign with him?

www.ingramcontent.com/pod-product-compliance
Lightning Source LLC
Chambersburg PA
CBHW060606230426
43670CB00011B/1988